# Industrial Archeology

Narrow gauge concrete rail ties, Hamakuapoko Sugar Mill ruins (1880), Paia, Maui, Hawaii

# Industrial Archeology

## A New Look

## at the American Heritage

THEODORE ANTON SANDE

I have not formerly been an advocate for great manufactories. I doubted whether
our labor, employed in agriculture, and aided by the spontaneous energies of the
earth, would not procure us more than we could make ourselves of other necessaries.
But other considerations entering into the question, have settled my doubts.

THOMAS JEFFERSON

## The Stephen Greene Press

BRATTLEBORO, VERMONT

## Illustration Credits

The photographs on the following pages were made by **Jack E. Boucher,** and are reproduced through the courtesy of the Historic American Engineering Record (HAER), National Park Service: facing page 1, 2, 5 (bottom), 6–7, 16, 18–23, 25–6, 44, 47, 51 (bottom), 52 (top), 56, 58–60, 63–4, 72 (top), 73 (top), 80, 92–3, 96 (top), 98, 99 (bottom), 102–15, 121, 127, 131, 134, 136–40, 144, 146, 151, back end-sheets.

For other pictures, the author acknowledges contributions by many individuals and institutions, including the following:

**Front endsheets**—Library of Congress, photo by J. Vachon; **Frontispiece**—Historic American Buildings Survey (HABS), photo by Jack Boucher; **pp. 3–4**—HAER; **p. 5**—(top) HAER; **pp. 8–9**—Oregon State Highway Division, Parks & Recreation Section; **pp. 10–11**—HAER; **page 12**—(top) The Smithsonian Institution; (bottom) HAER; **p. 13**—The Smithsonian Institution; **p. 14**—Wm. Edmund Barrett, Washington, D.C.; **p. 15**—(top) HAER; (bottom) The Smithsonian Institution; **p. 24**—Utah State Historical Society, from HAER; **p. 28**—(top) Library of Congress, photo by R. Lee; (bottom) Library of Congress; **p. 29**—Alan Pitcairn, from Grant Heilman; **p. 30**—(both) Library of Congress, photos by J. Vachon; **p. 31**—(top) Alan Pitcairn, from Grant Heilman; (bottom) FAR. MAR-Co., Hutchinson, Kansas; **pp. 32–5**—HAER, photos by Wm. Edmund Barrett; **p. 36**—photo by William H. Pierson, Jr.; **p. 37**—(top) Library of Congress, from HABS; **p. 38** (top)—photo by William H. Pierson, Jr.; **p. 38**—(bottom) Library of Congress, from HABS; **p. 39** (top)—photo by William H. Pierson, Jr.; **p. 39**—(bottom) Library of Congress, from HABS, photo by Jack Boucher; **p. 40** (top) —photo by William H. Pierson, Jr.; **p. 40**—(bottom left and right) Library of Congress, from HABS, photos by Jack Boucher; **p. 41**—Library of Congress, from HABS, photos by Jack Boucher; **p. 46**—HAER; **pp. 48–9**—HAER, photos by Wm. Edmund Barrett; **p. 50**—U.S. Department of the Interior, Bureau of Reclamation; **p. 52** (bottom)—HAER; **p. 53**—HAER; **pp. 54–5**—HABS (p. 55 center photo by Jack Boucher); **p. 57** (both)—Louisville Water Company; **p. 61**—The Smithsonian Institution, photo for HAER by Richard J. Pollak; **p. 62**—HAER; **p. 66**—American Precision Museum; **p. 67**—The Smithsonian Institution; **p. 68**—(left) photo by Allan Seymour; (right) The Smithsonian Institution; **p. 69**—photos by Allan Seymour; **pp. 70–1**—The Smithsonian Institution; **p. 72** (bottom)—HAER; **p. 73** (bottom)—HAER; **pp. 74–5**—Albert Kahn Associated Architects & Engineers, Inc., photos by Hedrich-Blessing Studio, Chicago; **pp. 76–7**—Albert Kahn Associated Architects & Engineers, Inc., photos by Forster Studio, Detroit; **p. 78**—(top) HAER, photo courtesy of Mr. John Gruber, Reading, Pennsylvania; (bottom) HAER, photo by Wm. Edmund Barrett; **p. 79**—HAER, photo by Wm. Edmund Barrett; **p. 82**—National Archives, Record Group 26; **p. 83**—HAER, photo by I. F. Brooks; **p. 84**—(top) San Francisco Port Commission; (bottom) HAER; **p. 86**—Library of Congress; **p. 87**—HAER, courtesy of Rensselaer Polytechnic Institute, Troy, New York; **pp. 88–9**—The Smithsonian Institution; **p. 90**—HAER; **p. 94**—National Register photo by Ron Walker, Courtesy of Missouri Department of Natural Resources; **p. 95**—HAER, photos by Wm. Edmund Barrett; **p. 96** (bottom)—HAER; **p. 97**—HAER; **p. 99** (top)—HAER; **pp. 100–1**—photos by Grant Heilman, Lititz, Pennsylvania; **p. 116**—The Smithsonian Institution; **p. 119**—Louisville Water Company; **pp. 124–9**—The Smithsonian Institution; **p. 133**—HAER; **pp. 142–3**—HABS; **p. 149**—HAER, photo by Wm. Edmund Barrett; **p. 152**—photo by William H. Pierson, Jr.

The photos on pp. 42–3 are by the author.

This book has been produced in the United States of America: designed by R. L. Dothard Associates, composed by American Book–Stratford Press, printed by Salina Press, and bound by Halliday Lithograph Corportion. It is published by The Stephen Greene Press, Brattleboro, Vermont 05301

LIBRARY OF CONGRESS CATALOGING IN PUBLICATION DATA
Sande, Theodore Anton, 1933–
    Industrial archeology: a new look at the American Heritage.
    Bibliography: p.
    Includes index.
    1. Industrial archaeology—United States.    I. Title.
T21.S26       609'.73       75-8196
ISBN 0-8289-0290-9

# Contents

# Industrial Archeology in America

*Industrial archaeology is a field of study concerned with investigating, surveying, recording and, in some cases, with preserving industrial monuments. It aims, moreover, at assessing the significance of these monuments in the context of social and technological history.*     R. A. BUCHANAN

For some time now, Americans have heard they live in a "post-industrial" age. The busy factories, mills, power plants, transport terminals, rail and highway grids that we see all around us are, we are told, of the past, not the future. Yet it is the spread of industry that formed the whole order of our society from the beginning years of the United States. Now, the post-industrial theory tells us, this spread has run its course, and we must recognize a new and vastly different set of principles.

Perhaps the growth of interest in industrial archeology in America over the past ten years is evidence that the prophets of the post-industrial age are right. We seem most willing to appreciate and learn from what has lately been lost.

Of course industrial archeology is not the only field in which the object of interest is the industrial past. Historians of economics, technology, and culture have explored a number of important questions pertaining to the industrial revolution and its aftermath. What distinguishes industrial archeology from these is its point of departure—the industrial site and its interpretation. This approach demands multi-disciplinary co-operation in order to comprehend the full range of past methods, production, working conditions, daily life, social patterns, economic organization—whatever. "Industrial monuments" (understood to refer primarily to fixed-in-place buildings, earthworks and machinery, or their remains) are to be explored, measured, recorded and, above all, placed in a *historical* setting.

It is this looking at the instruments and edifices of industrial society as culturally significant artifacts that is characteristic of industrial archeology, and it is this, too, that is relatively recent, especially in America. It would not have occurred to any of the men who built our modern industries to think of industry as the object of serious study for an array of persons, from scholars to enthusiastic amateurs, who call themselves industrial archeologists.

Indeed, until quite recently the rule has been for most people to regard objects like the ones that appear in this book as utilitarian embarrassments, to be ignored if possible, otherwise despised. This attitude is less evident today. We are reappraising the mills, factories, terminals, workers' housing and other structures that earlier generations looked at but, in a sense, never saw. We are learning to see them now, and find in them a whole new subject for appreciation and research. It is clear to us that industrial sites, old and recent, are essential parts of American history. For all that can be learned from them, they need to be recorded, analyzed, and preserved as carefully as the ancient townsites, artworks and cathedrals of more traditional archeology.

As more and more laymen, as well as historians, social scientists, architects, engineers and others, come to share this outlook, industrial archeology comes into its own. Through the international Society for Industrial Archeology, and in a growing literature, the field has already made an impressive start toward accumulating a useful body of knowledge on North American industrial history.

This book is intended as an introduction to American industrial archeology. Individual industrial sites are illustrated with some 150 photographs, drawings, maps and old engravings. Sites have been gathered into five categories, divisions of industrial activity that have been important throughout history: exploiting mineral resources; developing agricultural resources; producing energy; manufacturing; providing transportation.

The selection of sites does not follow any single plan. Some are here because they are representative, others are unique, still others have unusual beauty, or happen to be well documented and illustrated. The same applies to the list of American industrial sites in the appendix.

Those who know something of America's industrial archeology will be familiar with many of the places in this book, for many are already classics. But the reader new to industrial archeology—for whom this work is mainly intended—will, we hope, be sparked to pursue the subject further by the ingenuity, variety and grandeur of American industrial works that are displayed in this brief selection. Space has not permitted telling fully what transpired at any single site, and I have chosen to emphasize physical, visually prominent aspects because they are what one encounters first. But keep in mind that these structures are the result of human aspiration, inspiration and pain—that side you must also know to make the story whole.

Kennecott open pit mine, Utah

# Out of the Earth

Mining, and the allied activities that refine or otherwise modify what is mined, are the starkest and most arduous of all industries, requiring of their workers even today a pioneering spirit and the endurance of hardship. Mining sites are usually remote from civilized communities, which may pose great difficulties in transportation and construction. Building materials are often lacking and have to be brought in from great distances. Nevertheless, miners have been tireless builders. Perhaps no other enterprise furnishes a wilderness or a desert more quickly with shops, houses, mills, transport facilities, places for brawny entertainment, and other structures. For many sites in the West, mining operations have been civilization's advanced guard, though the amenities they offered seemed few.

In the nature of mining, the structures associated with it are frequently not built for posterity. When the ore is gone, miners do not linger. Remains of old mining operations are often scanty, but at the same time such structures as survive can be truly monumental— utilitarian splendors like the Silver King ore-loading station, and the Tintic standard reduction mill.

1

Silver King, north elevation

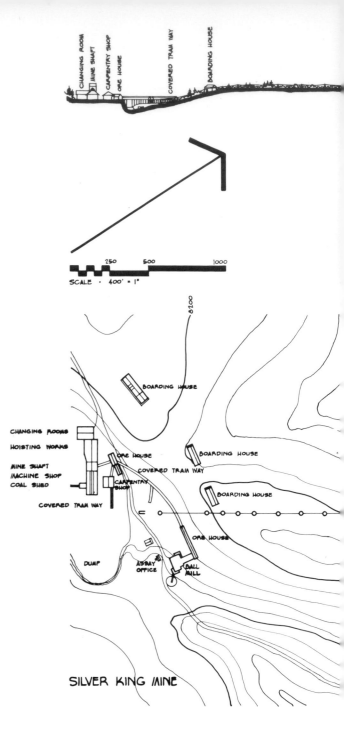

CHANGING ROOM
MINE SHAFT
CARPENTRY SHOP
ORE HOUSE
COVERED TRAM WAY
BOARDING HOUSE

SCALE · 400' = 1"
250    500    1000

8100

BOARDING HOUSE

CHANGING ROOMS
HOISTING WORKS

MINE SHAFT
MACHINE SHOP
COAL SHED

ORE HOUSE
COVERED TRAM WAY

BOARDING HOUSE

CARPENTRY SHOP

COVERED TRAM WAY

BOARDING HOUSE

ORE HOUSE

DUMP

ASSAY OFFICE

BALL MILL

SILVER KING MINE

# Silver King Ore-Loading Station

### PARK CITY, UTAH    1901

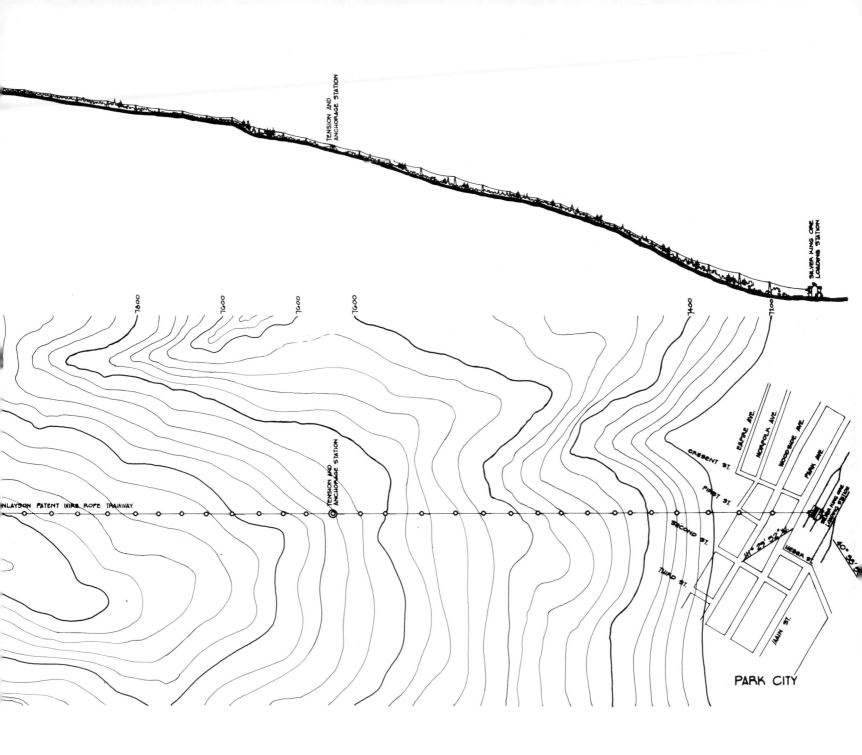

TENSION AND ANCHORAGE STATION

SILVER KING ORE LOADING STATION

7800 7700 7600 7500 1400 1300

INLAYSON PATENT WIRE ROPE TRAMWAY

TENSION AND ANCHORAGE STATION

SILVER KING ORE LOADING STATION

EMPIRE AVE. NORFOLK AVE. WOODSIDE AVE. PARK AVE.

CRESCENT ST.

FIRST ST.

SECOND ST.

THIRD ST.

MAIN ST.

MESSA ST.

114° 50' W.

40° 38' N.

PARK CITY

THIS HEAVY-TIMBER STRUCTURE looms at the end of a Union Pacific rail spur in the mining country southeast of Salt Lake City. The Silver King Mine was discovered in 1892. Its main shaft extended to 1,300 feet in depth, and was made up of three compartments. The map, above, shows the mine site, on the extreme left, with buildings—including three miners' boarding houses, an assay office, and shops. The line of the Finlayson-patent wire-rope conveyor or tramway

leads down to the ore-loading station at right.

Silver King was among the most successful silver operations in Utah, continuing in use as late as 1950. Since then, the mine has been largely abandoned, though recently there has been some work in the old shafts. Most of the above-ground buildings, including the ore-loading station, stand deserted or have burned. The wire-rope tramway was dismantled in 1971.

The illustrations give a sense of how the building

3

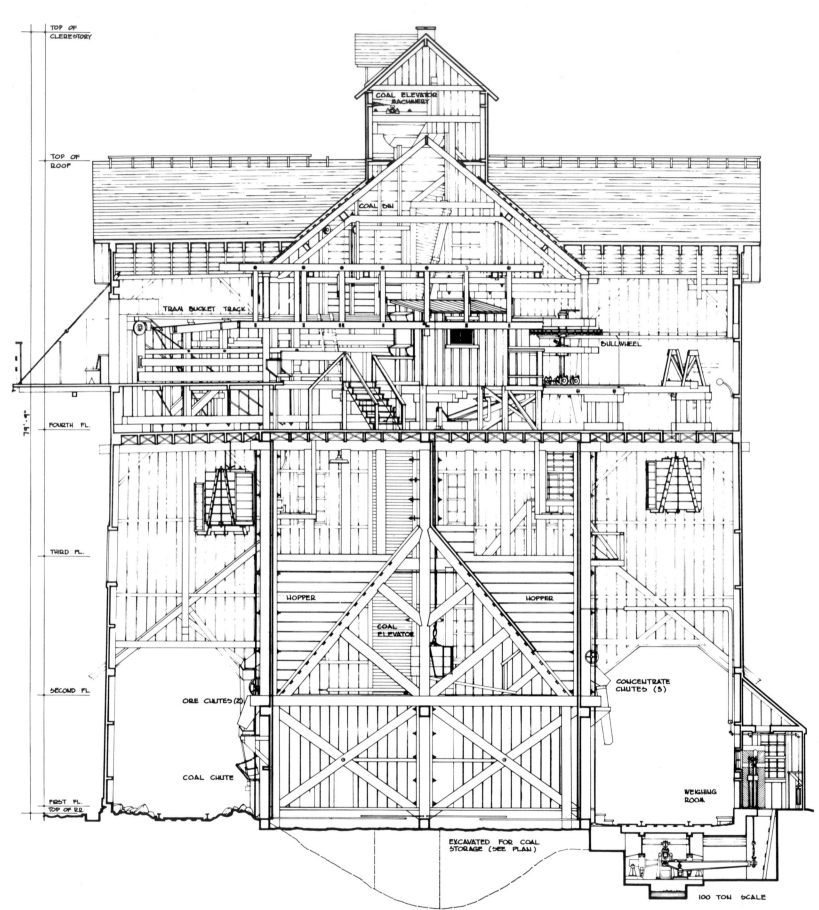

TOP OF
CLERESTORY

TOP OF
ROOF

COAL ELEVATOR
MACHINERY

COAL BIN

TRAM BUCKET TRACK

BULLWHEEL

79'-9"

FOURTH FL.

THIRD FL.

HOPPER                                    HOPPER

COAL
ELEVATOR

SECOND FL.                                          CONCENTRATE
CHUTES (3)

ORE CHUTES (2)

COAL CHUTE

WEIGHING
ROOM

FIRST FL.
TOP OF R.R.

EXCAVATED FOR COAL
STORAGE (SEE PLAN)

100 TON SCALE

4

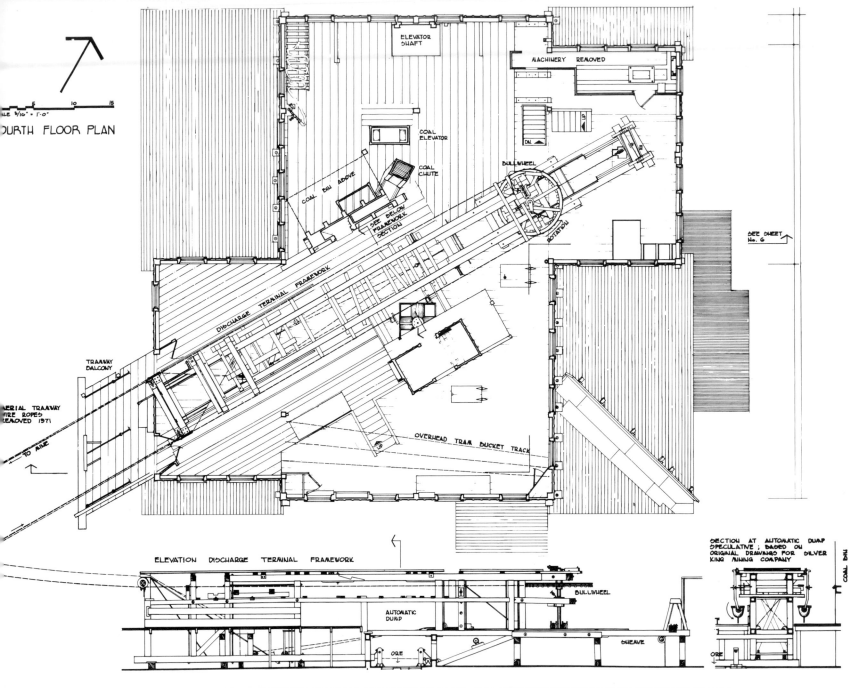

FOURTH FLOOR PLAN

SCALE 3/16" = 1'-0"

5 10 15

ELEVATOR SHAFT

MACHINERY REMOVED

DN

COAL ELEVATOR

COAL CHUTE

COAL BIN ABOVE

SEE BELOW FRAMEWORK SECTION

BULLWHEEL

ROTATION

SEE SHEET No. 6

DISCHARGE TERMINAL FRAMEWORK

TRAMWAY BALCONY

AERIAL TRAMWAY WIRE ROPES REMOVED 1971

TO MINE

UP

OVERHEAD TRAM BUCKET TRACK

ELEVATION DISCHARGE TERMINAL FRAMEWORK

AUTOMATIC DUMP

BULLWHEEL

SHEAVE

ORE

SECTION AT AUTOMATIC DUMP SPECULATIVE ; BASED ON ORIGINAL DRAWINGS FOR SILVER KING MINING COMPANY

COAL BIN

ORE

worked. The station was linked to the mine itself by the mile-long tramway, which carried newly-mined ore from the mine, which was located at 8,100 feet elevation, to the loading station a thousand feet below (see map). The tramway entered the ore-loading station at the fourth-floor level, indicated in the fourth floor plan on page 5 by the balcony that projects out at lower left. In the floor plan, again, the tramway is seen to enter the station on a diagonal. In the upper right of the plan is the bull-wheel around which the wire rope turned in its continuous counterclockwise journey to and from the mine. A detail of the bullwheel is shown on page 5, bottom.

The tramway originally ran by simple gravity: the weight of the ores descending from the mine gave the conveyor enough momentum to carry it back up to the mine loaded with fuel or supplies on the return trip. A steam engine may have taken over when the tramway did not run by itself.

Buckets attached to the tramway cable dumped ore from the top level of the loading station into hoppers. From the hoppers, the ore dropped through chutes into railroad cars drawn up below for shipment to the smelters. High-grade silver entered the station at the right-hand portal seen in the view of the north elevation on page 2; lower grade silver ores entered at a separate portal on the left.

At one point, the station was modified to transport coal to the mine. The cross section of the building on page 4 shows where the coal was stored under the first floor. From there it was drawn up by a vertical conveyor to the fourth level, to be loaded into the tramway's buckets and sent up to the mine. The fourth floor plan shows the added coal chutes, bins and elevators at the upper left.

The view at left shows the interior of the lower-grade ores portal. The chutes from the hoppers are on the right.

On the facing page is a view of the station's south side, showing the handsome heavy-timber framing of its exterior. The pattern of the timbers reflects precisely the lines of the hoppers' sloping undersides within.

# Sumpter Valley Gold Dredge No. 3

SUMPTER, OREGON    1935

NOW WORN BY twenty years of neglect, this gangling goose of a machine was part of a once widespread mining industry in eastern Oregon's Blue Mountains. It is the last of three "Yuba-type" gold dredges that were active in the Sumpter Valley from 1913 to 1954, when this one stopped in its tracks where we see it today.

No. 3's working lifetime amounted to fifteen years between 1935 and 1954 (it was shut down during World War II). The insatiable dredge ran day and night, served by three-man shifts onboard and others ashore, and produced an amazing $4.5 million worth of gold.

Essentially, No. 3 is a self-propelled barge on which machines are mounted. Designed for mining alluvial deposits, gold dredges like No. 3 scooped sand and mud from one side of a river or pond, and ran it through onboard machinery to sift it for precious metal. The sifted mud and sand were then dumped out on the other side of the stream. Chewing its way along a stream, as No. 3 did on the Powder River (shaded area on the map), a dredge left a path called a tailing. Like strip-mining, dredging operations wrought havoc on the terrain wherever they went.

Dredge No. 3 was designed by W. H. Cullers of the Boles' Shipbuilding Company of Portland, Oregon, and built right on the banks of the Powder River. Its hull, of West Coast fir, is 120 feet long and 52 feet wide. On the hull amidships are mounted a wood-sheathed, steel-frame housing containing sifting and related machinery, and, at either end, the digging equipment: a "stacker" and the "digging line."

The stacker is a 96-foot-long cylindrical prod, extending off to the right in the top picture. In use, it dipped its snout into the more easily worked soils and drew them up to the dredge using a 36-inch-wide conveyor belt inside the prod. The digging line at the opposite end of the dredge (at right in the lower picture) was a far tougher instrument. Its 72 buckets, each having a capacity of 9 cubic feet, could cut their way 13 to 16 feet down through hardpan to bedrock. The digging line ran at a speed of 20 to 25 buckets per minute. It was powered by a 250-horsepower electric motor.

All deposits brought to the surface by the digging equipment were flushed through revolving screens on the dredge. These sifted out everything under 3/4-inch in diameter. One 6-inch and two 10-inch pumps provided flushing water at a rate of 8,000 gallons per minute.

In addition to No. 3 itself, two trucks, two tractors, machine shops, a sand house and an office were required to run this dredging operation on the Powder River. All but the dredge have been removed.

Gold dredging came to a standstill in the Sumpter Valley in 1954, when the miners formed the plan of extending digging into portions of the town of Sumpter. Word of the project leaked out prematurely, causing drastic increases in local real estate prices. The project was stopped, and No. 3 has been idle ever since. At last report, plans were underway to restore and convert it into a mining museum.

# Oil Rig

## VOLCANO, WEST VIRGINIA

### ca. 1895–ca. 1899

THESE WOOD-FRAME oil derricks and other buildings, standing in a West Virginia woodland, are rare survivors of a type of oil well pump that was fairly common in its time. Installations like these were distinguished by the way power was transmitted to each pump.

A central power source—in this case a one-cylinder, 20-horsepower, internal-combustion engine that burned natural gas—drove an "endless-wire" cable that ran from it to each well, eventually returning to the engine to begin its circuit again. This arrangement meant that only one engine was needed to run several wells (at a time before electric power was readily available, the alternative was for each well to have its own power source—an expensive undertaking). Employing a single, central prime mover also saved manpower; one or two men could run several wells.

The system was invented in the 1870s by W. C. Stiles, Jr., who apparently got the idea for a cable-drive system from observing how power was then being transmitted in Philadelphia machine shops. Later a portion of the oil well pumping system was modified to run a lever-

arm pump motivated by an eccentric located on the driver wheel of one of the main pumps. This second pump was known as a "Jack wheel." It was in wide use in the early days of the Texas and Oklahoma oil fields.

The photograph opposite shows the modified pumping apparatus. The horizontal walking beam is connected to the large wheel's crank on the right. This wheel, when it turns, rocks the beam up and down, driving the pump's piston rod (at the left). The cable's linear motion is thus changed to rotary motion at each well by the wheels, and then changed again to pumping motion by the pumps' crank-driven walking beams. The derrick shown above was constructed to hold pipe lengths in place over the wells during drilling operations. Others were used to extract pipe and rods from wells for replacement.

Today, as old-style wells need new equipment, the original structures are gradually being dismantled and the old pumps are superseded by electric motors. A proposal recently made by the Oil and Gas Memorial Committee of West Virginia's Antiquities Commission would include the Volcano site as part of a state park.

# Coke Ovens

ELEVATION

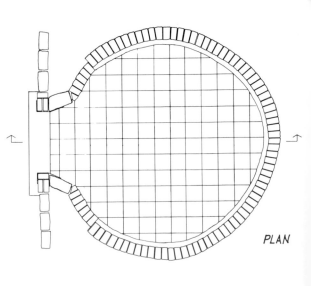

PLAN

LONG RIBBONS of low masonry walls, pierced every fifteen feet or so by gaping doorways, can be found nestled into hillsides along railroad tracks in western Pennsylvania and West Virginia. They are the old ovens in which soft coal was burned to turn it into coke, the best fuel for smelting iron ore.

The value of coke as a fuel in smelting was discovered in England in the early 1700s. In the United States, the production of coke on a large scale dates from about 1850, though the Oliphant Furnace near Uniontown, Pennsylvania, used coke successfully as early as 1837.

The ovens pictured, all in West Virginia, are of the "beehive" type. Originally, coke was produced simply by piling coal in mounds and burning it in the open air. Use of the beehive oven began to replace open-air coking as early as 1763 in the British coke industry, though the ovens pictured here all date from early in this century. By 1900, there were about 7,300 ovens like these in operation in West Virginia alone.

On page 12 is a photograph of the abandoned battery of ovens at Richard, West Virginia, which date from 1904–5, and below are measured drawings of one of the ovens at this site. Notice in this picture that the ovens' situation, on a hillside or bank, allows only a single row

of ovens. On more level ground, ovens could be placed back-to-back in a staggered arrangement that used space more efficiently. Immediately below is an early 1900s view of the Mercury Coal and Coke Company's works at Bretz, West Virginia, where coking dates back to about 1906.

Beehive ovens were usually about 12 feet in diameter and 7 feet high inside. They were built of firebrick and clay mortar, and had iron-frame doorways. The dome shape made for a rigid structure, and served to focus heat on the coal loaded within.

Ovens were charged from the top by a special hopper or "larry car." The coal was then leveled by a man with a hand rake who thrust it back and forth inside the oven from outside the doorway. The door was sealed with temporary bricking, leaving a small space above the coal at the top of the doorway for air supply. It required about 48 hours of burning to turn a normal charge of $4\frac{1}{2}$ to 5 tons of coal into coke.

On page 14 a detailed view of the interior of a typical beehive coke oven, built at the Elkins Coal and Coke Company in 1903, looks up toward the charging hole. The iron-frame doorway of an oven at the Cascade coke works (page 15) dates from about the same time.

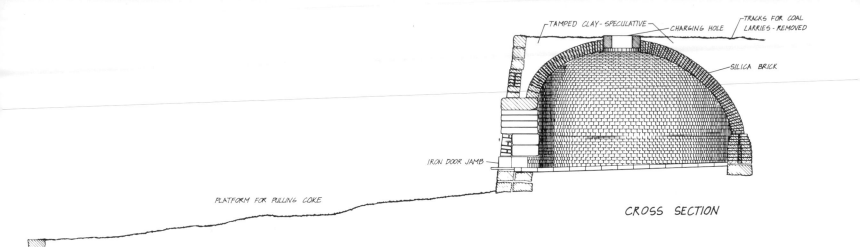

TAMPED CLAY-SPECULATIVE — CHARGING HOLE — TRACKS FOR COAL LARRIES-REMOVED

SILICA BRICK

IRON DOOR JAMB

PLATFORM FOR PULLING COKE

CROSS SECTION

In the transformation of coal into coke, volatile constituents in the coal are burned off and escape as gases. Although they were an important improvement over the old open-air cokers, beehive ovens were still wasteful, for the gases released by the coking process were lost. Today, the old beehive ovens have largely been replaced by more efficient by-product ovens, or coal-gas retorts, that recover the burned-off gases and put them to use.

15

# Tintic Standard Reduction Mill

**GOSHEN VICINITY, UTAH   1920**

SOUTH OF PROVO, Utah, this dramatic site appears off the highway about midway between the towns of Santaquin and Goshen. It is a splendid concrete ruin that cascades down a dry hillside.

Here, fifty years ago, newly mined ores were milled to separate out silver, copper, lead and gold. The ores were brought by rail to the mill, where they were raised to its uppermost level on an inclined tram. In successive stages of the refining process, ores were passed along down the hillside, from one level to a lower one (see section drawing, opposite). The Tintic mill's refining

16

method, known as the Augustin process, crushed the ore to about $\frac{1}{8}$-inch pieces in two Allis Chalmers roller mills. The crushed ore was baked in Holt-Dern roasters, then leached in a strong brine solution. The metals were finally separated in a copper precipitate process. Each batch of ore took approximately six days to process.

The Tintic mill was designed and built in 1920–1 by W. C. Madge at a cost of $580,000. It seems to have been the only ore-reduction mill built at this time to employ the by then outdated Augustin process.

The mill began operations in February, 1921, and

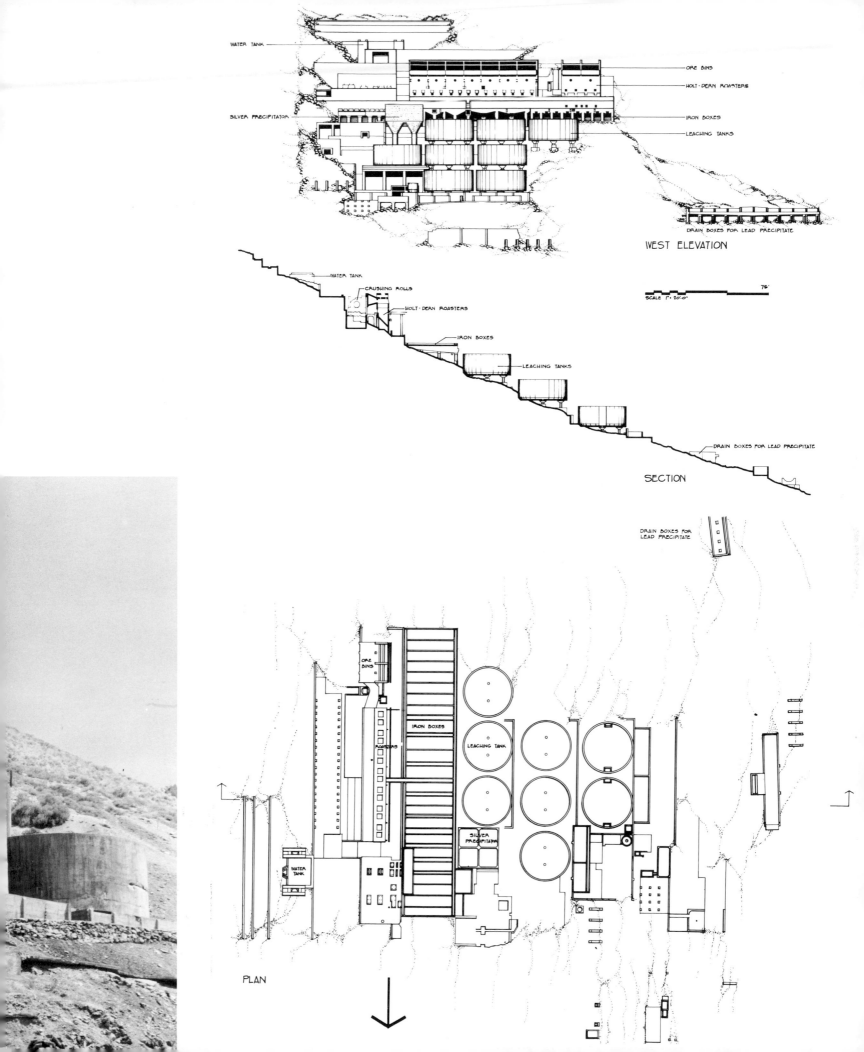

WATER TANK

ORE BINS

HOLT-DERN ROASTERS

SILVER PRECIPITATOR

IRON BOXES

LEACHING TANKS

DRAIN BOXES FOR LEAD PRECIPITATE

WEST ELEVATION

WATER TANK

CRUSHING ROLLS

HOLT-DERN ROASTERS

IRON BOXES

LEACHING TANKS

DRAIN BOXES FOR LEAD PRECIPITATE

SECTION

SCALE 1"=20'-0"     75'

DRAIN BOXES FOR
LEAD PRECIPITATE

ORE
BINS

IRON BOXES

ROASTERS

LEACHING TANK

SILVER
PRECIPITATOR

WATER
TANK

PLAN

soon reached full capacity, handling nearly 200 tons of ore per day in three 25-man shifts that kept the mill going around the clock. The mill's recovery rates for metals were relatively good (88 percent of the silver in ores was recovered, 60 percent of the copper, 32 percent of the lead, and 7 percent of the gold). However, the company's mine could not supply the mill with enough ore of the grade and composition that the mill's design required, and the operation was closed in 1925. It was dismantled a few years later, though the Tintic mine continued in operation, sending its ores directly to the smelter.

# Sloss Blast Furnaces

BIRMINGHAM, ALABAMA    1882–3

BLAST FURNACES are large fire-containers used for smelting ores. These two at Birmingham were for iron production, and their design is typical.

The furnace was charged at the top with iron ore, coke for fuel, and additives (fluxes) to aid in the smelting process. These were passed up to the furnaces along the steep conveyors that rise beside them in the views above and to the left. Near the furnace base, a series of blast holes, called *tuyères* (pronounced "tweers") were placed around the furnace's circumference. Air was mechanically blown through the *tuyères* to force combustion.

Inside the furnace, the iron melted, releasing impurities from the ore that combined with the coke's carbon to produce waste gases and slag. The heavier wastes, or "clinkers," settled to the bottom of the furnace, from which they had to be removed from time to time. Lighter wastes rose to the surface of the molten iron and were skimmed off before the iron was tapped out of the furnace near the base. Blast furnaces could remain in continuous operation for months, producing one batch of iron about every 12 hours.

In the construction of blast furnaces like the Sloss Furnace Company's, in the illustrations, exterior metal plates encase brick walls with firebrick linings. The walls of the Sloss furnaces are 27 inches thick. There are 10 *tuyères* in each furnace. Blast air came from large blowers. In these pictures the row of stacks between the two furnaces rises from ovens where incoming blast air was preheated by heat from furnace gases before being introduced into the furnaces.

Sloss built its Furnace No. 1 on an 18-acre site in Birmingham in 1882. No. 1 is the oldest blast furnace still standing in the area. A second was built the following year. Each furnace is 144 feet high.

Much of the old Sloss installation, though modified, still remains. The original developer, Colonel J. W. Sloss, sold the firm in 1886, but it continued under successor companies until the U.S. Pipe and Foundry Company finally closed it in 1970. The firm was reportedly forced to close down the Sloss works by the high cost of newly required antipollution devices.

In addition to the two furnaces, the Sloss site presently contains a powerhouse, engine rooms, boilers, a chemical laboratory, cooling towers, rail lines and offices. Now owned by the Alabama State Fair Authority, the site is on the list of threatened American industrial monuments: plans for its demolition are going forward.

# Mining Ghost Town

## MERCUR, UTAH    1869, 1895, 1933

THIS MINING TOWN—a ruin today—has lived and died three times. In 1869 gold was found in the area. The town, then named Lewiston, sprang up quickly and attained a population of 2,000. It thrived through the '70s, then faded as the rich gold-bearing ores were exhausted. By 1880, Lewiston was a ghost town.

About that time, a prospector named Pinedo working the area discovered cinnabar, the native sulfide from which mercury is refined. There was still gold, too, though it was bound up with its ores so tightly as to be

inaccessible to the smelting techniques then available. Mercury and gold revived the dead town, and gave it a new name—*Mercur*, Portuguese for "mercury." By 1890 several new mines had opened, and mills were being set up in the area to extract the gold from Mercur's tenacious ore. One mill was established that used electricity transmitted from a distant power plant. It was the first such mill in the country to use electrical power. By the turn of the century, when the old photograph on this page was made, Mercur was prospering.

24

The town burned to the ground in 1896, and again in 1902. Fire was a great danger in the tent-and-board boom towns of the arid west. After each disaster, however, Mercur, was speedily built up again.

By 1910, Mercur was a city with schools, churches, an opera house and good hotels. The population approached 12,000. But gold production began to fall off again. In 1913 the mines and mills began to close. By 1917 Mercur was deserted.

Its last rise began in 1933, when mining interests re-opened some of the old workings to wring still more gold from them through applying updated extraction processes. This time, although the mines revived, the town did not. Few permanent buildings were built; the men who worked the mines came to Mercur from cities near by. The latest workings at Mercur closed during World War II.

Today the foundations of the old mill buildings, a few falling-down shacks, derelict pieces of equipment, and the old trestle structures, are virtually all that remains of Mercur. On this site, the industrial archeologist must rely on old photographs, written accounts, and rigorous site excavation and recording, rather than on abundance of surviving buildings and machinery, to furnish material for his intellectual reconstruction of the past.

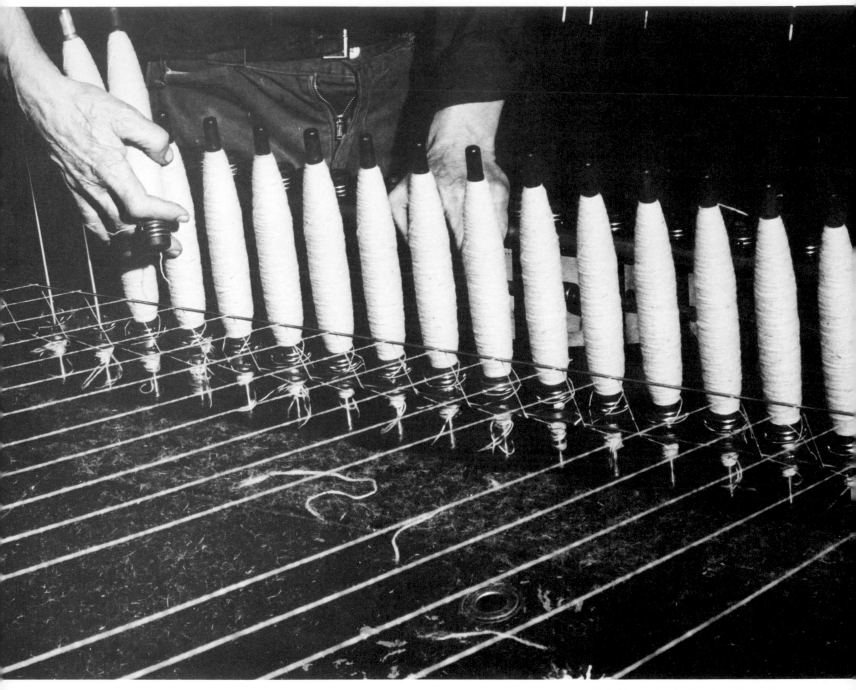

Spindles at Harrisville, New Hampshire

# From Plants
# and Animals

Many industrialists in the United States and elsewhere, and many more farmers, once believed that industry and agriculture were basically incompatible. The antagonism of factory and farm has not been much stressed among us recently, perhaps because in the last hundred years we have become more and more obviously an industrial country and less and less an agricultural one. Nevertheless, the division can perhaps still be felt in the class of industries that participate in agriculture.

Industrial life organized around products derived from plants and domesticated animals presents a calm and gentle aspect, contrasting with the raw power of mine and smelter. Even colossal grain elevators have about them a sense of repose. These are structures that are thoroughly controlled and well arranged in all their parts; there is nothing unclear in the elevators' shapes to confuse our visualizing what goes on inside them. All the industries that are based on agriculture—from paper mills to breweries to woolen mills—have in common the appearance of being orderly, well-run enterprises proud of the skills they employ and the products they make.

27

Wheat elevators, Latah County, Idaho (1941)

Small farm elevator, Cass County, North Dakota

# Grain Elevators

GRAIN ELEVATORS are focal points of large-scale Midwestern agriculture. They dominate the grain states' endless plains, leading some to call the larger elevators "prairie castles."

There are "country" elevators and "terminal" elevators. The difference between the two is mainly one of size. Country elevators serve nearby farmlands directly. They range from storage capacities of 100,000 bushels to capacities of about 2 million bushels. Terminal elevators are major regional grain collecting centers, which receive grain from many surrounding country elevators, and they are considerably larger than the latter. For example, FAR-MAR-CO's Hutchinson, Kansas, elevator (opposite) has a capacity of more than 17 million bushels contained within a structure almost a half-mile long and 127 feet high. It receives grain from southwest Kansas, Colorado, and northern Oklahoma.

28

Elevators at Texhoma, Texas (1942)

Country and terminal elevators work in about the same way. Grain is brought to the elevators by trucks or railroad cars, and dumped into a pit from which it flows (usually through a controlled passage or gateway) into a central "boot." It is then conveyed to distributors, located at the top of this central element, known as the "headhouse." From the distributors the grain is sent on to preselected storage bins, its eventual destination depending on the variety and quality of specific grains. The distributors may also send grain into scale bins where

Cressbard, South Dakota (1942)

Terminal elevators, Abilene, Kansas

it is weighed, and then sent on to storage, or into waiting railroad cars for immediate transport.

The distributors dispense the grain by means of fast-moving conveyor belts, housed in a long, low capping structure called the "gallery" or "Texas house," which rides over the tops of the storage bins for the full length of the elevator (below). As the grain approaches its designated place, a tripper throws it off the conveyor belt into a spout, through which it pours into the appropriate bin.

Terminal elevators can mix various grains to meet specific customer specifications. The elevator's head-house is the nerve center, containing (in addition to the distributors) scales and the elevator manager's control station.

The construction of the elevators must be such that the huge bins are water-, bird-, and rodent-proof. Accordingly, the two dominant types of elevator construction are reinforced concrete and wood-frame with a steel covering.

31

# Brew Houses

BREWING was an important industry in nineteenth-century America, as it is today. The process involves steeping malt (*i.e.*, barley grains whose starch has been converted into sugar) in water and then boiling it in brew kettles together with other ingredients, notably including hops. The resulting liquid is mixed with yeast and placed in large vats, where it ferments. The finished beer is drawn from these vats and stored until mature and ready to be drunk.

Nineteenth-century brew houses, like banks of the time, were apt to put on architectural airs. The styles in which they indulged themselves were often elaborate and eclectic.

In Baltimore, the American Brewery's five-story, brick-and-stone brew house is an unusually rich mixture, a concoction of the German Romanesque, French Second Empire and Italianate designs. The building was constructed in 1887 by an unknown architect for John Frederick Wiessner, a German immigrant who had been making beer on the site since 1863. When completed, Wiessner's new brewery was reported to have an annual production capacity of 100,000 barrels. Since 1973, the brew house has been closed.

Below, an interior view shows some of the brewery's machinery (since dismantled and removed): in the background is a Griffith and Wedge (Zanesville, Ohio) Cor-

liss-type steam engine that drove the F. W. Wolf (Chicago) refrigeration compressor in the foreground (used for chilling the finished beer).

## DENVER, COLORADO 1890–1

In Denver, the Tivoli (originally Milwaukee) brew house continued production from 1890 into the mid-1960s, with a hiatus during Prohibition. The building is now vacant. Brew houses are such highly specialized structures that it is hard to find other uses for them. These two interior views give a sense of what the Tivoli was like when in full operation. Above, a mixer stands behind a row of copper taps. Opposite, in a general view looking toward the main entrance side, hot water tanks are on the upper level and a mixing vat is at the intermediate, at left. Copper brew kettles are out of sight below. In keeping with the opulent brewery architectural tradition is the quatrefoil pattern of the decorative iron stair risers, and the curvilinear motif of the railings.

# Textile Mills

## HARRISVILLE, NEW HAMPSHIRE    1832–50

HARRISVILLE, a small mill town in the foot-hills of southern New Hampshire, enjoyed a modest prosperity in the nineteenth century, and today is an eloquent reminder of the industrial villages common in pre–Civil War New England.

Harrisville began its industrial career in the early 1830s. It grew, following the fits and starts of the national economy, until the end of the nineteenth century, then quietly subsided. The Cheshire Mills closed in 1971.

The mills of Harrisville made woolen cloth. The process of that manufacture consists of three principal steps: preparation of the wool, spinning, and weaving. Raw wool is first combed and carded to remove foreign matter, straighten the fibers, and align them for subsequent steps. The fibers then go through a series of spinning and drawing machines that twist and pull them into yarn strong enough to be woven. The yarn is finally woven into cloth on automatic looms.

The Harris Mill (page 38, top) was constructed about 1832. As the early view of the town (opposite, top) shows, the mill, at the left, was originally shorter than it is today, and lacked the present tower. The Harris Mill was superseded by the Cheshire No. 1 Mill, which began operations in 1850. Both mills span the Nubanusit River, which drove waterwheels centrally located in the mills' basements. Initially, all the mill machinery was water powered. The lower view on page 38 shows what remains of the original Harris Mill's iron gate-control mechanism, which regulated the flow of water to the wheel.

Cheshire No. 1 Mill (page 39, top), the only granite building in town, was built in 1847 for Cyrus Harris by a Rhode Islander, Asa Greenwood, but was not fully equipped and running until three years later. It is a handsome example of a type of textile factory that appeared in southern New England at a slightly earlier date.

36

EXISTING PLAN

C CHESHIRE MILLS OWNERSHIP

H TOWN OWNERSHIP

No. 1 has a more efficient attic arrangement than the Harris Mill's, the continuous strips of windows in No. 1 admitting more light for working (page 40, top). Notice, too, the "spinning mules" tucked away under the window sills in the interior of No. 1 (page 39, bottom). The mules were used to stretch and twist yarns in the process of making them strong enough for weaving.

Also evident in the attic view are pairs of wrought-iron tension rods in the center of the room. These were attached to the roof trusses and to the attic floor beams,

thus permitting open floor space for machinery, uninterrupted by support columns, on the second floor below. Structurally, Cheshire No. 1 is more advanced than the Harris Mill. The heavy-timber beams and thick wood-plank floors in No. 1 are considerably more fire-retardant than the simple wood-frame interior of the older building.

On page 40, the Cheshire No. 1 Mill is at the top, its reservoir in the foreground. Below it are detail views of the floral cast-iron fire stair, presumably added late in

38

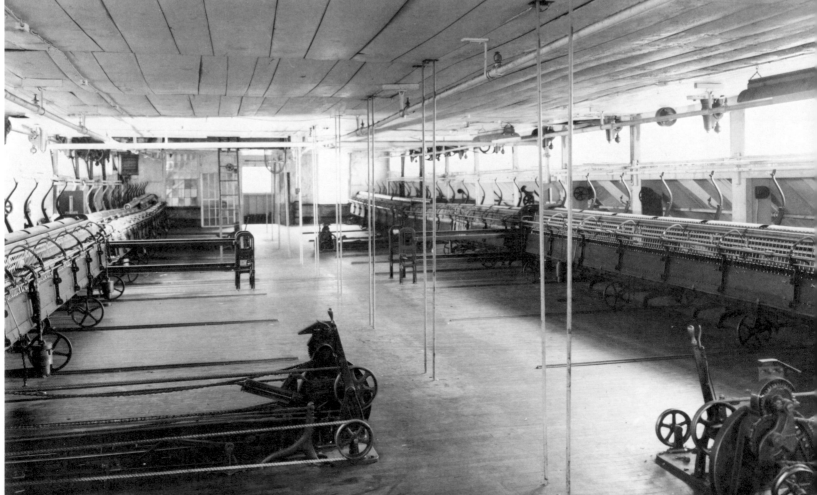

the nineteenth century, and the waterfall at the eastern extremity of the mill site.

In Harrisville's early days, the town's factories employed mainly single men and women, who lived in boarding houses. One that remains is the Cheshire Boarding House, above, located across the street from the mill's entrance. To the right is one of a number of distinctive structures associated with the mills, in this case a storage building.

Now a historic district, Harrisville recently has gained new life from the take-over of three old mill buildings by a manufacturer of industrial water coolers and filters. A maker of wooden toys has also moved onto the site, and a small-scale woolen operation has started in one of the older buildings. The village is, therefore, a prime example of the collective preservation of a complete industrial site, and of the preservation of old structures through adapting them to new uses.

# Pejepscot (Topsham) Paper Mill

**TOPSHAM, MAINE    1868**

THE TOPSHAM PAPER COMPANY put up this mill building in 1868 on the banks of the Androscoggin River at Brunswick Falls, a site that had been used for water power by various enterprises since the 1700s.

The handsome old mill is of restrained Italianate design. Its three-and-a-half story brick walls bear on a granite foundation and inclose a heavy-timber interior structure. Although the interior machinery has been removed, the mill still serves as a storage building for the Pejepscot Paper Company.

Paper is made from fibrous cellulose materials. Straw, linen and cotton rags were the principal raw materials for paper making until the nineteenth century, when the size of the reading public grew, increasing the demand for paper. Paper manufacturers needed a more abundant source of material; they found it in wood pulp.

In the 1870s, a chemical process was developed that allowed wood to be broken down into pulp for paper manufacture. Wood chips were boiled with soda or sulphite solutions (making very unpleasant odors) to remove impurities such as resin. Large amounts of clean water were needed, which favored locating pulp mills near fast-flowing rivers.

Earlier, in 1798, the paper industry had been significantly advanced by the French, who invented machinery for manufacturing paper in continuous lengths instead of single sheets. A process evolved in which wood pulp and other materials were poured in a thin layer onto a moving web, where the fibers bonded into a uniform sheet that was then drawn off the rollers for drying.

The Pejepscot is the oldest remaining wood-pulp paper mill in Maine. The mill building is distinguished in its architectural treatment, especially on the southern elevation (opposite), which is marked by a system of arched bays, defined by recessed brick panels of varying heights and pierced by arched windows. The site includes, besides the brick mill, a large number of wooden buildings. The interior of one of these is seen above, with modern equipment in place.

The wood-pulp paper industry began to assume importance at Topsham—and elsewhere in the region—after 1874 when the mill was acquired by the Bowdoin Paper Manufacturing Company. The company's treasurer, Adna T. Denison, saw the potential of wood-pulp paper manufacturing, and led the way in its early development as one of the principal industries of the State of Maine, and of northern New England generally.

Windmill, Nantucket, Massachusetts

# Power and Services

No branch of industrial activity affords more variety of type and scale of enterprise than the class of structures, old and new, built to produce and conduct power, from whatever source. Power for industry has come from small wind- and water-mills that yielded no more driving power than a single team of horses or oxen, and from huge hydroelectric dams and power plants that supply the complex electrical distribution grids we depend on today.

In history, no factor has influenced the development of American industry more than the availability of water power. Of the older factory sites included in this book, the majority were originally located to take advantage of nearby rivers or streams. In the last hundred years steam and electricity, and the internal combustion engine, have freed industry from dependence on water power, and so have helped to permit factories to thrive in all kinds of localities across the country.

45

# Eclipse
# Railroad
# Windmill

**SHEFFIELD, TEXAS    1898**

FOR THE INDUSTRIAL archeologist, this huge windmill is of interest from several points of view: as a stationary machine; as an integral part of steam-powered transportation in the nineteenth century; and as an example of a machine's being put to another specific use.

Steam locomotives of the 1800s required frequent water replenishment for their insatiable boilers. Water stops had to be at regular intervals along the line. When the railroads were built across the dry flatlands of west Texas in the 1880s, windmills like this one provided the water they needed. Wind flow, translated into mechanical power by the mill, drove a deep water pump. The mill's tail or rudder, projecting out to the right in the illustration, kept the blades headed into the wind.

Many of these railroad windmills were taken over later by farmers and cattlemen of the region for watering livestock. This one, located on the Cannon ranch, is unusually large, having a blade diameter of 22½ feet. It is said to be the largest windmill made by the Eclipse Wind Engine Company, a major manufacturer and supplier located in Beloit, Wisconsin. The tower was replaced in 1915, and the windmill itself was restored in 1964.

46

# Bronson Windmill

**FAIRFIELD, CONNECTICUT**
**1893–4**

THIS IS a far more complicated, and a more stylish, windmill than its West Texas counterpart. It was custom-built to supply water to a large dairy farm on a private estate, and was part of a substantial building program initiated here in 1891 by financier Frederic Bronson II. Bronson selected the fashionable architect Richard Morris Hunt to design the mansion on his estate, and he seems to have had equally grand intentions for his windmill, which was designed by Andrew J. Corcoran, maker of the Corcoran "Storm-Defying" windmills.

The structure is framed in Georgia pine, and has shingled siding and a candlesnuffer roof. The 80-foot octagonal tower contains a large wooden tank. There is also an underground cistern. A windlass turned the mill to engage the wind.

The Bronson mill is no longer in use, and needs repair. It is owned by a private school.

47

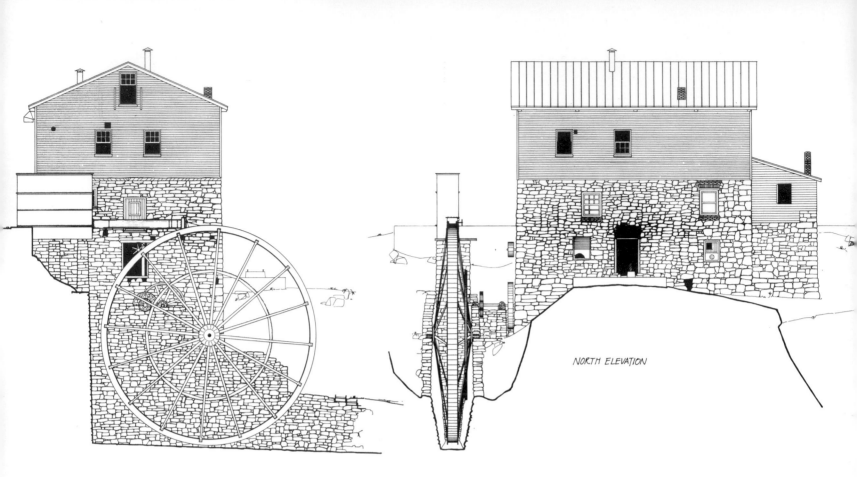

NORTH ELEVATION

# Gristmill

**SHEPHERDSTOWN, WEST VIRGINIA    ca. 1734–9, 1890, 1905**

SHEPHERD'S MILL is representative of the water-driven gristmills that were so common in the American Colonies, and so important in their local economic order. Today, the site is significant because it shows modifications made over the years to adapt the structure to advances in grist milling and water power technology.

In the late 1700s, fifty years after Thomas Shepherd built this mill, the famous millwright Oliver Evans introduced a conveyor system that largely automated the process of moving grain in the mill through the various stages that eventually transformed it into flour. Others improved upon Evans' invention through the nineteenth century, but it was only in the late 1870s that a central-European method of milling a finer, better flour was adopted that used chilled iron rollers in place of grind-stones. We can see this technological change reflected at Shepherd's mill. The new technique required greater

power than the old, posing a serious problem for owners of low-powered rural water mills who wanted the improved machinery. Some millers changed from water to steam power; others substituted a water turbine for the wheel, or installed more efficient wheels. At Shepherd's mill, the third course was taken. Roller machinery was apparently installed in the early 1890s. The wrought-iron "overshot" waterwheel shown in the pictures, 40 feet in diameter, dates from the same time. The wheel was first located 150 feet downstream from the mill, the water being brought to it by a metal trough mounted on a timber trestle. Power was transmitted from the wheel to the mill by an endless-wire belt. In 1905 the waterwheel was moved to the mill building and installed where the original wooden wheel had stood.

The wood-frame third floor of the mill undoubtedly was built atop the original stone structure at the time the iron rollers were installed.

48

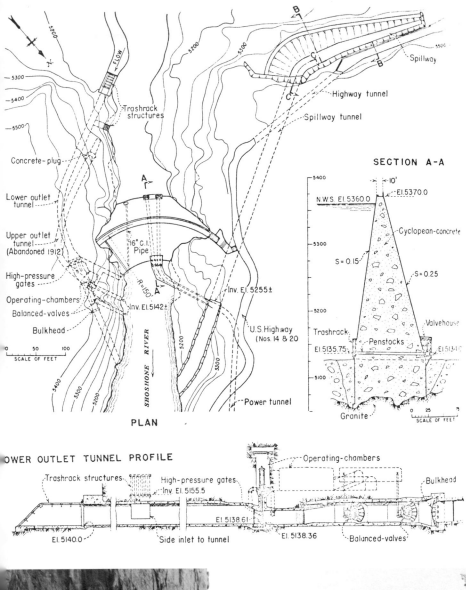

SECTION A-A

PLAN

POWER OUTLET TUNNEL PROFILE

# Buffalo Bill Dam

## CODY, WYOMING 1905–10

THE CONCRETE of the Buffalo Bill (formerly Shoshone) Dam is smoothly cut into the weathered stone cliffs of the Shoshone River gorge in northwestern Wyoming. This was one of the first high concrete dams in the United States. It was built to store the river's flood waters in a 6,710-acre reservoir. The water was subsequently used for irrigation and to generate electric power.

The dam was named after Colonel William F. Cody, "Buffalo Bill," the famous wild-west showman, who was an advocate of irrigation for the arid region. The Shoshone River dam project now irrigates about 94,000 acres.

Built on a so-called "constant radius" design, the dam is 325 feet high, and tapers from a 108-foot thickness at its base to a thickness of 10 feet at the top. It has a volume of 82,900 cubic yards. Near the dam's base is the 5,600-kilowatt Shoshone power plant (1922).

51

# Mountain Dell Dam

MOUNTAIN DELL RESERVOIR

**PARTLEY'S CANYON, UTAH**
**1914, 1924**

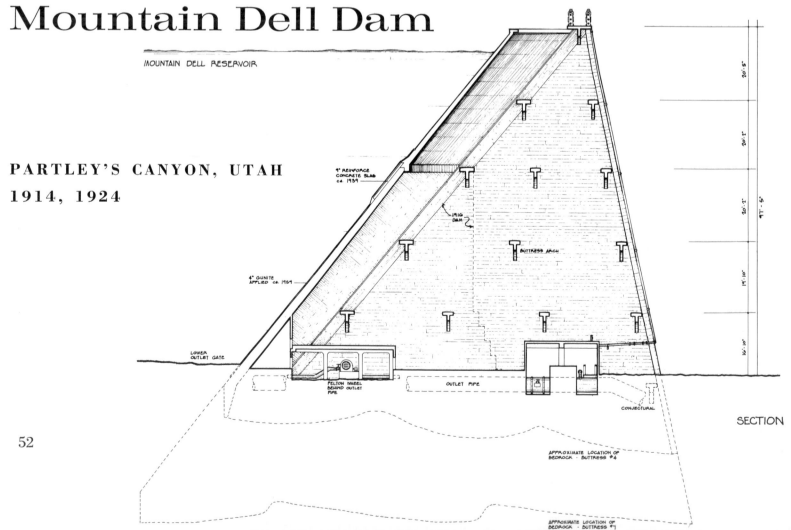

9" REINFORCE
CONCRETE SLAB
ca. 1939

1916
DAM

BUTTRESS ARCH

4" GUNITE
APPLIED ca. 1939

LOWER
OUTLET GATE

FELTON WHEEL
BEHIND OUTLET
PIPE

OUTLET PIPE

CONJECTURAL

SECTION

APPROXIMATE LOCATION OF
BEDROCK · BUTTRESS #4

APPROXIMATE LOCATION OF
BEDROCK · BUTTRESS #7

52

ANOTHER WESTERN DAM, this one located northeast of Salt Lake City, is an early example of a reinforced concrete dam in the innovative multiple-arch design developed by John S. Eastwood, who built nineteen of these in various parts of the world.

By slanting the arches and pier buttresses (see section drawing opposite), Eastwood achieved a structure that resisted both overturning and sliding at its base; in fact, the dam has increased stability under increased loading. The dam's multiple-arch design was especially suited to sites with unstable bedrock conditions.

The buttresses of the Mountain Dell Dam, set on centers 35 feet apart, originally enclosed 11 bays. In 1924, ten years after it was built, the dam was increased in height from 105 to 145 feet; the increase added five bays at the top.

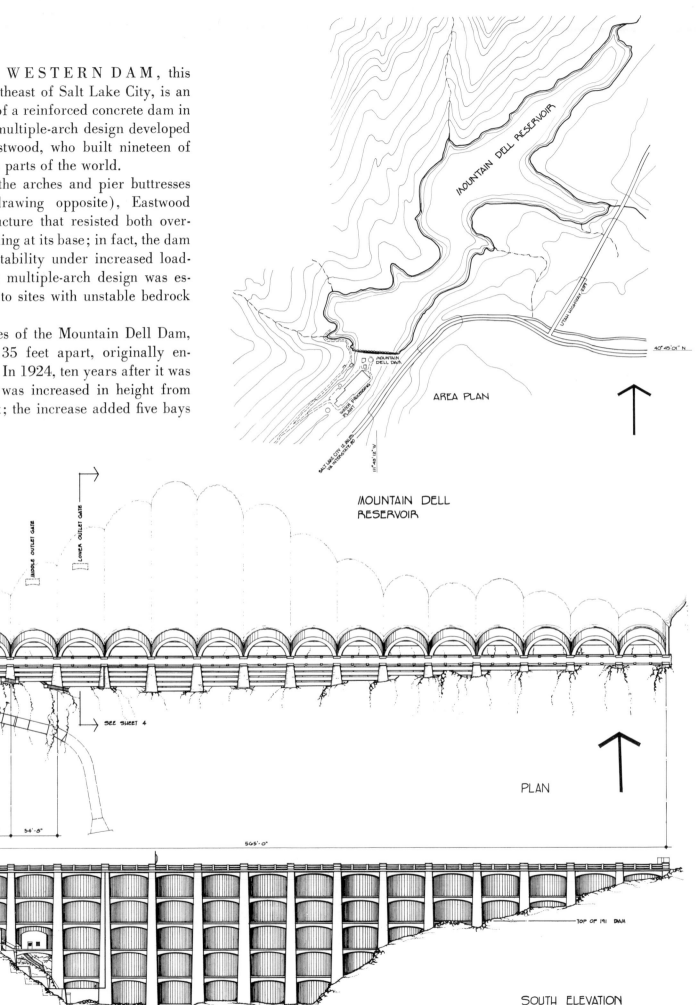

AREA PLAN

MOUNTAIN DELL RESERVOIR

PLAN

SOUTH ELEVATION

# Adams Power Plant

## NIAGARA FALLS, NEW YORK    1895

WHEN IT BEGAN operations, on August 5, 1895, the Adams Station was the world's first large-scale producer of alternating electric current. Nationally, alternating current made it possible for central generating stations to supply large areas. The Adams power plant, in particular, gave impetus to the Niagara Falls electrochemical industry by furnishing ample electric power at low cost.

The Niagara Falls power plant system developed in the 1880s with a plan, devised by Thomas Evershed, to build a system of 12 canals, drawing water for mechanical power from the upper river, and capable of supplying 238 water-wheel pits. Once used, the water was to be discharged into the gorge of the Falls by way of a tunnel to be built under the city (see map at right).

Edward D. Adams, after whom the power plant station was ultimately named, was the president of the construction company that was to build the system. Seeking advice on how best to develop local water power resources, Adams organized an international competition in 1891, in which experts were invited to submit plans. The only point of agreement that emerged was that 5,000-horsepower generators were the best size for making electricity. There was no consensus on a method for power distribution. Construction eventually followed a plan, based on Evershed's original mechanical power scheme, that employed the best features of the entries submitted.

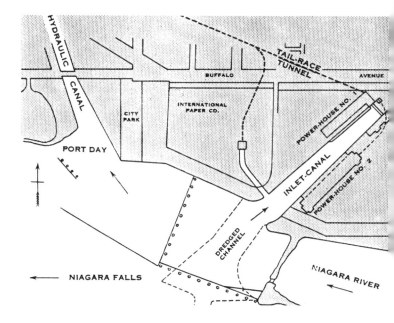

By December, 1892, the main tunnel under the city was completed. The problem of distributing the electric current that the system was to generate was finally solved by adapting a new plan for electrical generation, distribution and use developed independently by George Westinghouse and exhibited at the World's Columbian Exposition in Chicago in 1893.

When completed, the Niagara Falls site had the world's first 5,000-horsepower electric generators (one of which is seen opposite, upper right) the first synchroscope (a device for keeping alternating current generators in step), and a handsome collection of masonry buildings designed by the famous New

54

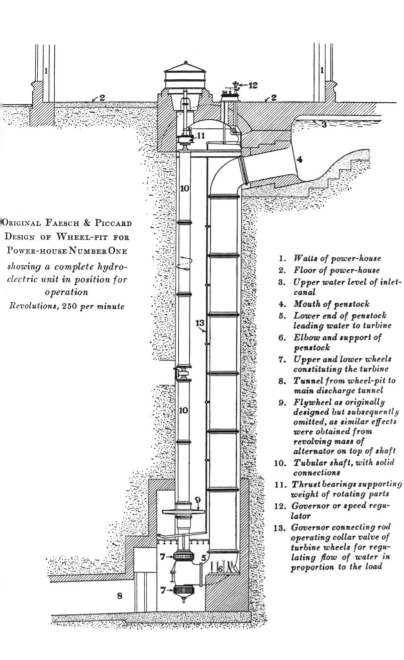

ORIGINAL FAESCH & PICCARD
DESIGN OF WHEEL-PIT FOR
POWER-HOUSE NUMBER ONE

*showing a complete hydro-
electric unit in position for
operation*
*Revolutions, 250 per minute*

1. *Walls of power-house*
2. *Floor of power-house*
3. *Upper water level of inlet-canal*
4. *Mouth of penstock*
5. *Lower end of penstock leading water to turbine*
6. *Elbow and support of penstock*
7. *Upper and lower wheels constituting the turbine*
8. *Tunnel from wheel-pit to main discharge tunnel*
9. *Flywheel as originally designed but subsequently omitted, as similar effects were obtained from revolving mass of alternator on top of shaft*
10. *Tubular shaft, with solid connections*
11. *Thrust bearings supporting weight of rotating parts*
12. *Governor or speed regulator*
13. *Governor connecting rod operating collar valve of turbine wheels for regulating flow of water in proportion to the load*

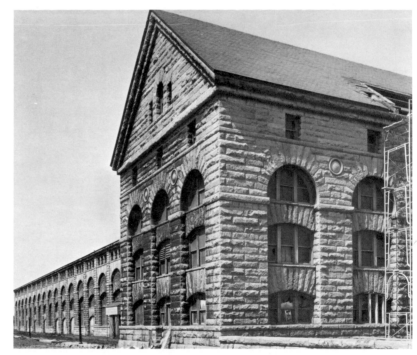

York architects McKim, Mead and White. This most significant historic site has been demolished over the last ten years, and a stone entrance portal is all that remains of it today.

# Louisville Water Company Pumping Station

## LOUISVILLE, KENTUCKY    1860

AT THE END of Louisville's Zorn Avenue stands this arresting pumping station in a classical temple motif, combining elements of ancient Greek and Roman architecture with later Renaissance themes. Theodore R. Scowden, the Louisville Water Company's chief engineer, designed the station in two parts: an engine room and boiler house, and a standpipe tower. The engine room is the two-story temple itself, with its Corinthian portico and dual one-story wings. It originally contained two batteries of boilers (three Cornish boilers in each), two pairs of duplex steam pumps (see drawing at right), and two Cornish beam engines (the beams of which are shown in the lower picture). Offices and other facilities were housed in the wings. The standpipe tower, a 169-foot Doric column capped by a round temple and embellished at its base with a Corinthian colonnade, is built of brick up to the tops of the colonnade's statues. The construction is riveted steel plates and sheet metal above this point. Of the ten statues on the colonnade, nine are derived from classical mythology; the tenth is of an American Indian with his dog.

The Louisville pumping station initially had a capacity of 100,000 gallons of water per day, drawn from the Ohio River and sent through about 26 miles of pipe to 500 customers.

In 1890 a tornado blew the standpipe tower down. The city quickly replaced it. Three years later a new pumping station was built next to the original one. Although the 1860 building is no longer in use and its machinery has been removed, it is still well maintained by the Louisville Water Company.

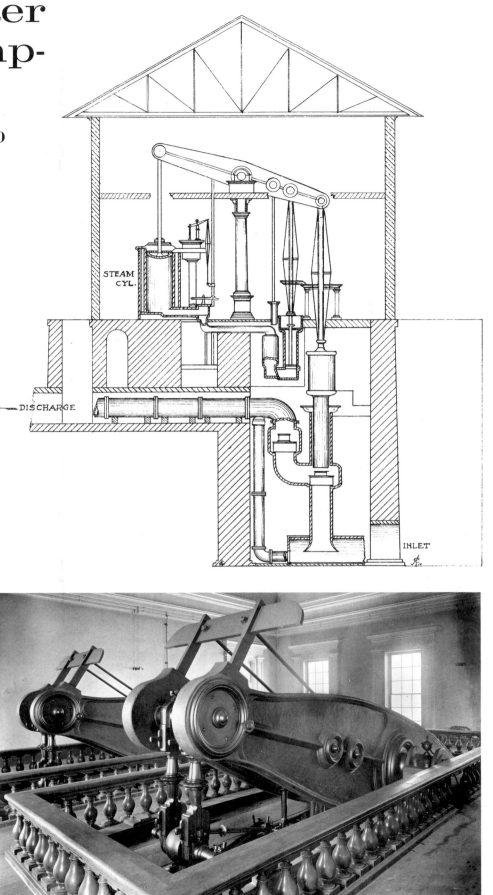

# Gasholder House

**TROY, NEW YORK    1873**

GASHOLDER HOUSES were common in New England and upstate New York in the 1870s and '80s. Of the twelve that survive in the region, the most impressive is this one, built by the Troy Gas Light Company in 1873.

Gasholders are expansible structures. Their iron tanks (which we still see today held by open metal frameworks) consist of a telescoping section, which, when empty, rests within a pit of slightly larger diameter. In old-type gasholders, the pit was filled with water. This

58

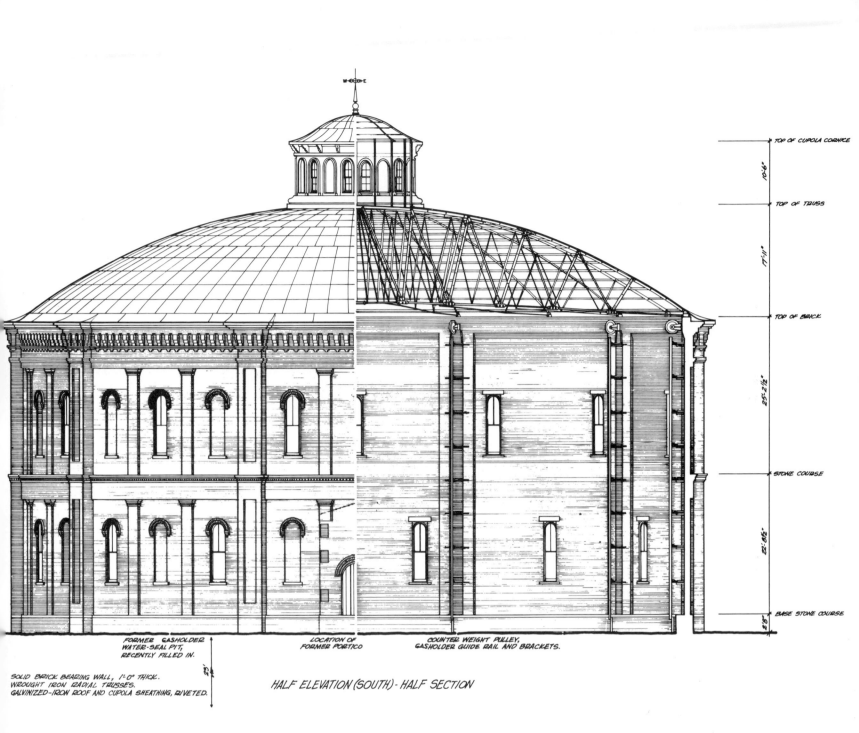

TOP OF CUPOLA CORNICE

10'-6"

TOP OF TRUSS

17'-11"

TOP OF BRICK

25'-2½"

STONE COURSE

22'-6½"

BASE STONE COURSE

2'-3"

FORMER GASHOLDER
WATER-SEAL PIT,
RECENTLY FILLED IN.

LOCATION OF
FORMER PORTICO

COUNTER WEIGHT PULLEY,
GASHOLDER GUIDE RAIL AND BRACKETS.

SOLID BRICK BEARING WALL, 1'-0" THICK.
WROUGHT IRON RADIAL TRUSSES.
GALVINIZED-IRON ROOF AND CUPOLA SHEATHING, RIVETED.

HALF ELEVATION (SOUTH) - HALF SECTION

created a seal, and prevented gas from escaping where the pit and the iron tank met.

When exposed to the hard winters of the Northeast, however, the water was apt to freeze in the pit. Hence the gasholder house, designed to solve this problem by protecting the gasholder itself from winter freezing, ice and snow. Enclosing the gasholder also eliminated wind pressure and other loads on it, permitting thinner iron plating to be used in its construction, which in turn allowed freer

movement of the telescoping section. Gas condensation in cold weather was also reduced by the partial temperature control that the gasholder house afforded. The cupola atop the wrought-iron-truss roof was for ventilation.

The Troy gasholder house was designed by a prominent gas engineer, Frederick A. Sabbaton. Its gasholder had a capacity of 300,000 cubic feet. Although this building is constructed of brick (see ornamental work,

59

above and opposite), some other gasholder houses were stone, or were wood-frame.

The Troy structure is no longer used to shelter a gasholder. Its interior brick pit has been filled up to grade level, and the north wall has been opened to admit trucks and other vehicles. Its present owner, a painting contractor, stores heavy equipment in the building.

Because of the uniqueness and quality of this structure, a drawing of it has been adopted by the Society for Industrial Archeology as the organization's symbol.

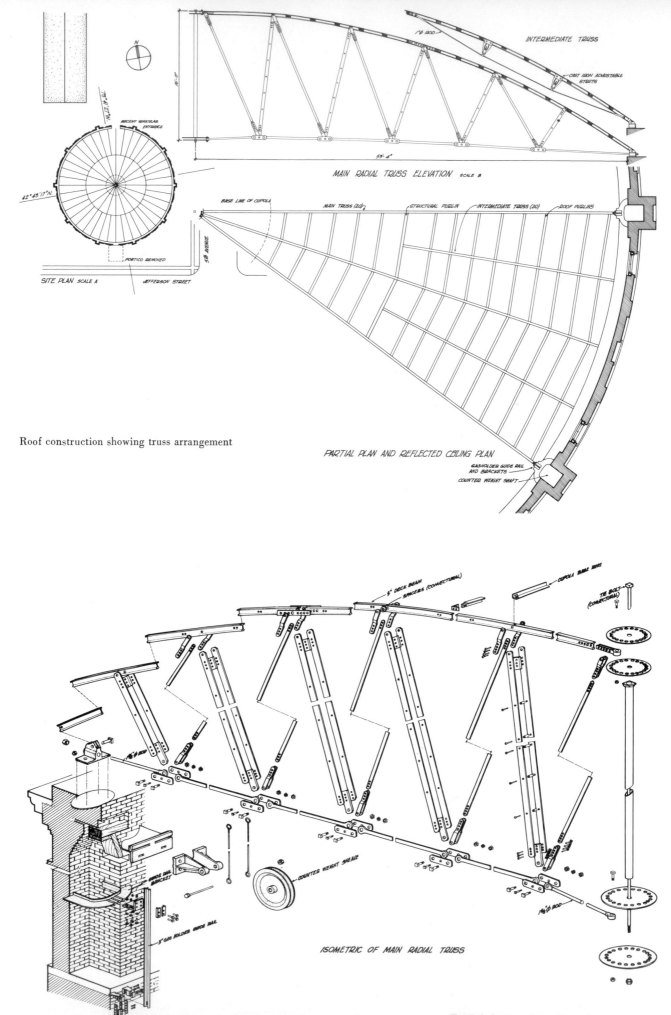

INTERMEDIATE TRUSS

CAST IRON ADJUSTABLE STRUTS

MAIN RADIAL TRUSS ELEVATION SCALE B

RECENT VEHICULAR ENTRANCE

N

PORTICO REMOVED

SITE PLAN SCALE A

JEFFERSON STREET

BASE LINE OF CUPOLA   MAIN TRUSS (20)   STRUCTURAL PURLIN   INTERMEDIATE TRUSS (20)   ROOF PURLINS

Roof construction showing truss arrangement

PARTIAL PLAN AND REFLECTED CEILING PLAN

GASHOLDER GUIDE RAIL AND BRACKETS

COUNTER WEIGHT SHAFT

DECK BEAM

SPACERS (CONJECTURAL)

CUPOLA BASE RING

TIE BOLT (CONJECTURAL)

GUIDE RAIL BRACKET

COUNTER WEIGHT SHEAVE

GAS HOLDER GUIDE RAIL

ISOMETRIC OF MAIN RADIAL TRUSS

62

Exploded view of a main roof support truss

Woodward Iron Works, Woodward, Alabama

# Manufacturing

America has always been proud of its factories, and ready to boast of their feats of manufacturing. Carl Sandburg wrote that

*An Ohio man bundled up the tin roof of a summer kitchen and sent it to a motorcar maker with a complaint of his car not giving service. In three weeks a new car arrived for him and a letter: "We regret delay in shipment but your car was received in very bad order."*

Among the six manufacturing sites treated here, the Gruber Wagon Works is separated from the Dodge Assembly Plant by fifty years and several revolutions in production methods and technology. Nevertheless, each, in its time, was dedicated to turning out the most improved product, through the use of the most advanced equipment and techniques.

65

# Robbins & Lawrence Machine Shops

WINDSOR, VERMONT    1846

Lyman gun sight machine (1835)

THIS ELEGANT FACTORY stands on the bank of Mill Brook in the small town of Windsor, on the western bank of the Connecticut River. Windsor is note-worthy in American industrial history for the products made in this building since before the Civil War. The shop, built of hand-made bricks and topped with a splendidly proportioned cupola, was initially an armory and machine shop for the firm of Robbins, Kendall & Lawrence (Kendall sold out in 1847).

The factory's early claim to fame came in 1851 when six of the company's military rifles were shown at the Great Exhibition in the Crystal Palace, London. The Ver-mont rifles received a medal of excellence; the judges, and British Army officials, were particularly impressed by the weapons' interchangeable parts.

Robbins & Lawrence eventually received substantial military contracts from the British government. The first contract was for 138 machines—mostly milling ma-chines—for making the latest-model Enfield rifle-musket. Later, under pressure from the Crimean War for more weapons, the British placed another contract with Rob-bins & Lawrence, this time for 25,000 Enfield rifles. This contract, however, proved to be the firm's undoing. Overextended financially, and unable to meet deadlines, the company defaulted in late 1856 and was taken over by the British in June of 1857.

In 1858 the old Robbins & Lawrence shops were sold

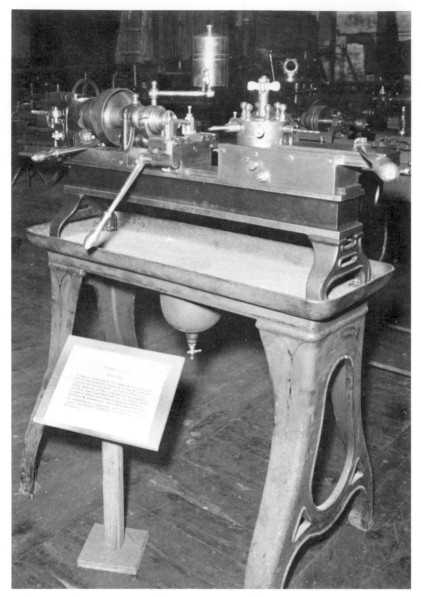

Engine lathe (ca. 1885) of the type made in the factories

Hendey shaper (1876)

to Lamson, Goodnow & Yale, which made in succession over the next thirty years Springfield rifles for the Union Army, cutlery, cotton textiles and machine tools.

After 1888, the Windsor Machine Company made high quality turret lathes in the factories. In 1910 the Windsor Company moved to a new location, and the old factory began a fifty-year career as an electric power station.

The structures seen on the right in the nineteenth-century lithograph of the site (preceding pages) were demolished for tenement housing after the First World War. Notice the rifle weathervane, symbolic of the firm's premier product in its early years. Also, in the top picture opposite, note the continuous window-strips let into the roof, and compare them with the structurally more complicated lighting arrangement in the attic of Harrisville, New Hampshire's Cheshire No. 1 Mill on page 40.

The main building was acquired by a non-profit educational corporation in 1966, and now houses the American Precision Museum, and an important collection of tools and machines (opposite, below). The building was designated a National Historic Landmark in 1966.

# Colt's Armory

## HARTFORD, CONNECTICUT  1864

ALSO ON THE CONNECTICUT River, but a hundred miles south of Windsor, Vermont, is Samuel Colt's famous armory. Today the armory is surrounded by much taller buildings, but its blue onion-shaped dome still commands attention. In the old woodcut of the site, we see that the armory once dominated the river bank.

In 1836 Colt, a Hartford native then twenty-two years old, organized the Patent Arms Company in Paterson, New Jersey, to exploit his invention of a firearm whose cartridges were held in a cylindrical magazine that revolved, allowing it to be fired several times without reloading between shots. Colt was ahead of his time, however, and the Paterson factory closed in 1842. Colt then went on to other projects, notably the development of the first successful marine telegraph cable. Five years later, he returned to firearms, prompted by a request from General Zachary Taylor for a thousand revolvers for the Mexican War. Colt made the guns in Eli Whitney's Whitneyville, Connecticut, armory. In late 1847, he leased a three-story wood-frame building in Hartford, and went back into arms manufacture, this time with great success.

In 1852, Colt purchased 200 acres of land in the South Meadows of Hartford, where he built the world's largest privately-owned armory, and a workers' village, completed in 1855. The armory building burned, and the present factory replaced it in 1864.

Although Colt died in 1862, his armory continued to prosper. In the Civil War, it supplied the Union Army with more than half a million revolvers, muskets and rifles. Since then, a number of advances in weaponry have been made at Colt's armory, including the famous Gatling Gun, 10 crank-operated revolving barrels capable of firing 1,000 rounds per minute, making it the first "machine gun." The armory is still very much in use today.

On the facing page, a recent photograph of the armory, and an earlier woodcut, show that the main building has been extended and modified at the ends and roof. The building's interior has an unusual combina-

tion of machinery and structure. The Porter-Allen steam engines (1864) seen above have been placed vertically, their crankshafts (one of which is seen in the picture between the massive cast-iron support struts) connected to the overhead line shafting. In addition, as the picture shows, the horizontal line shafting is supported by the big cast-iron struts, which also extend above the shafts to become structural columns for the girders of the floor above.

71

# Rogers Locomotive Erecting Shop

PATERSON, NEW JERSEY    1871

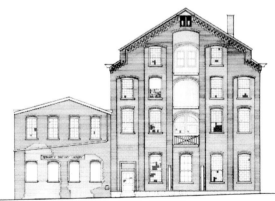

NORTH ELEVATION

## ROGERS ERECTING SHOP

THE ROGERS LOCOMOTIVE AND MACHINE WORKS ERECTING SHOP IS LOCATED ON LAND ORIGINALLY LEASED FROM THE S.U.M. BETWEEN 1851 AND 1856. THE FIRST BUILDING ON THIS SITE WAS USED AS A FOUNDRY FOR THE FACTORY (NO LONGER IN EXISTENCE) ACROSS THE STREET. THE PRESENT BUILDING REPLACED THIS AND OTHER STRUCTURES ON THE PROPERTY IN 1871. THE MAIN BUILDING CONSISTS OF A BASEMENT (NOW FILLED), THREE FLOORS, AND A LOFT. SEVERAL SUBSEQUENT ADDITIONS HAVE BEEN MADE TO THE 1871 STRUCTURE.

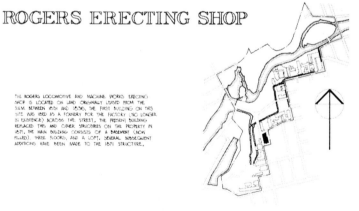

WEST ELEVATION

THOMAS ROGERS came to Paterson at a time when the city was prospering from a heavy demand for textiles during the War of 1812. By the early 1830s he was making structural components and engine parts for railroads, and by 1836 he had started making locomotives. By 1840, the Rogers firm was turning out railroad steam engines at a rate of about seven a year. After Rogers' death in 1856 the firm began to decline.

The locomotive erecting shop shown on the facing page was built in 1871, and originally consisted of 12 bays. Over the years a number of changes were made in the building. Such modifications are typical of factory buildings, in which space requirements change as production increases or new methods are introduced. The interior construction of the Rogers plant consists of wood floors and joists supported by heavy-timber girders and cast-iron columns (see section drawings below). Locomotive components were made on the upper floors. The locomotives themselves were assembled on the ground floor.

73

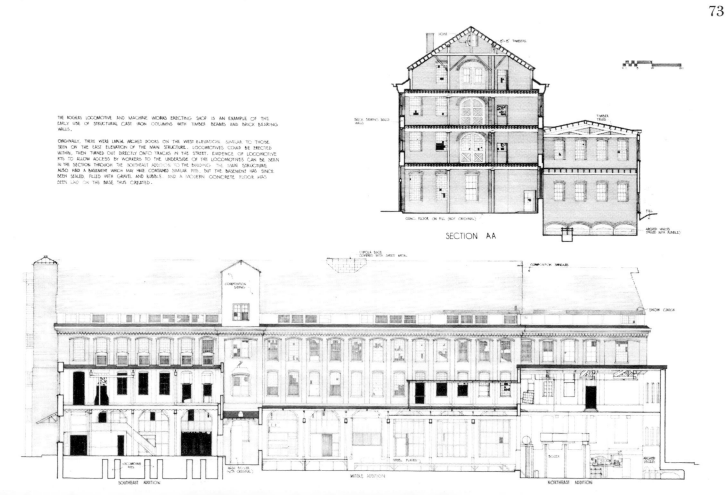

# Dodge Half-Ton Truck Assembly Plant

**DETROIT, MICHIGAN 1938**

CHOSEN IN 1944 by the Museum of Modern Art as one of the outstanding examples of American architecture, this factory embodies in a distinctive building some of the characteristic features that recent manufacturing techniques demand in factory construction. All phases of production are located on the same floor to make the operation move swiftly and efficiently. The interior space of the building is relatively free of upright

supports and other structural members (see above), allowing machinery to be rearranged as needed with little disruption. The factory also admits large amounts of sunlight, increasing visibility and creating pleasant working conditions.

All these improvements were first made possible by the development of structural steel, which allowed factories to take the form of a thin, very strong steel skeleton, uncluttered on the inside and having only a lightweight skin of brick and glass wrapped around it to keep out the weather. Opposite, an exterior view shows the Dodge's radiator grille in the foreground, its parallel lines having seemingly been picked up and turned vertically in the glass walls of the factory itself.

The Dodge truck plant is also of special interest as an architect-designed building. Before the Civil War most factories were designed and built by the combined efforts of millwright and owner. Later, factories were designed by men who frequently styled themselves "mill engineers." The industrial architect appears only occasionally before the beginning of this century.

Albert Kahn, who designed this building for the Dodge Division of Chrysler Corporation, was a pioneer in modern industrial architecture.

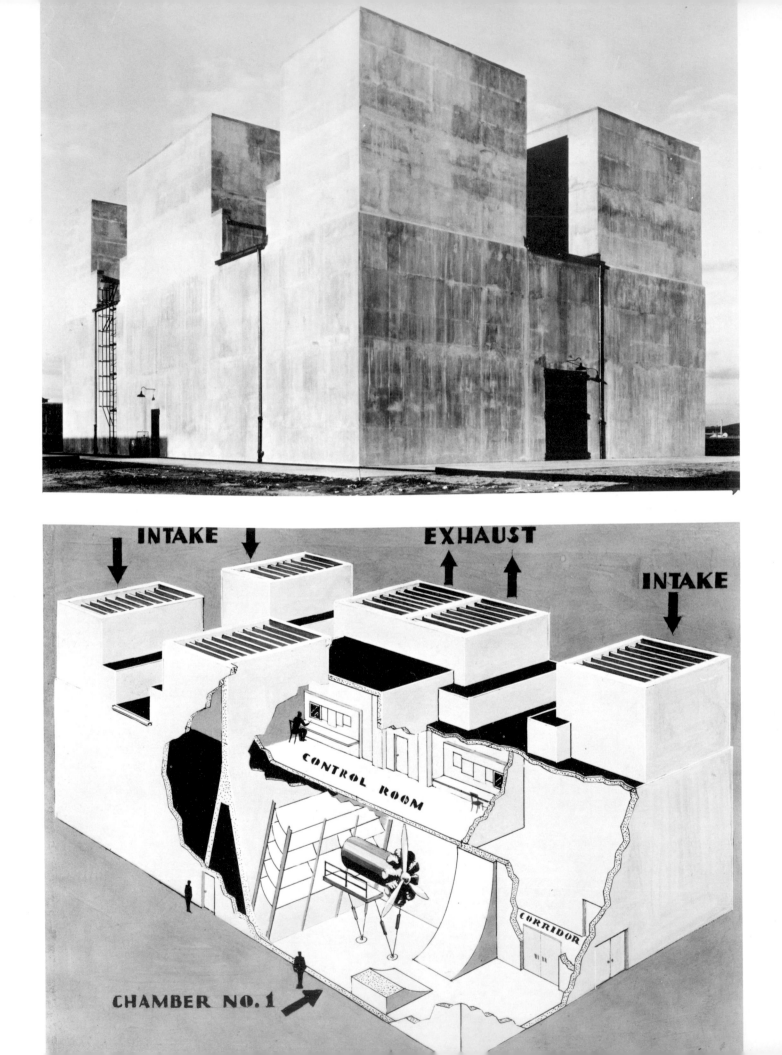

# Pratt & Whitney Engine Test House

**EAST HARTFORD, CONNECTICUT   1937**

ANOTHER of Albert Kahn's industrial buildings differs considerably from his Dodge truck plant. At the Pratt & Whitney building, there is no skeleton framing or thin exterior wall. Instead, the building is a massive structure, designed for a specific and highly specialized purpose: testing aircraft engines. Heavy reinforced concrete walls rise in six towers to give the building a monumentality that suggests some long forgotten civilization.

As a comparison between the exterior view and the diagram below it shows, the structure of the engine test house has been carefully worked out to achieve sound-proofing. To avoid disturbing neighboring operations when engines were run at full speed, the test house had to be as soundproof as possible.

In the view below, taken in 1937, an engine is shown in place ready for testing. The turnbuckle cables are used to suspend the engine in the opening, allowing air to flow freely on all sides.

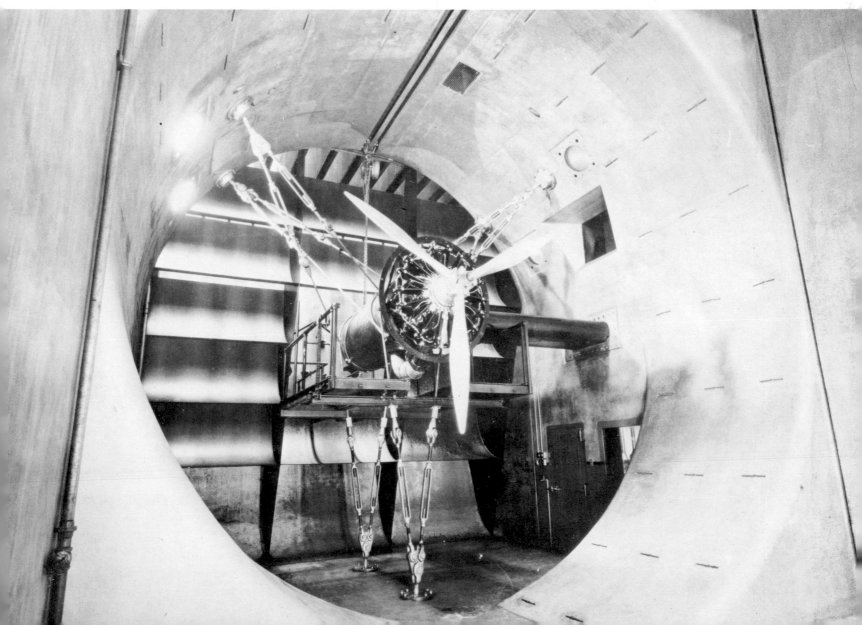

# Gruber Wagon Works

THIS UNPRETENTIOUS two-story wood-frame building is one of the best examples in the United States of the type of rural manufacturing common in the late nineteenth and early twentieth centuries.

The firm was started in 1854 by Isaac Gruber, and grew steadily into the post–Civil War period. It continued until the 1920s, and even in the 1950s did wagon repair work. The building is now unoccupied. This, the firm's second building, was erected in 1882, and has been added to a number of times since then.

The factory is divided into three rooms on the first floor: blacksmith, wood and bench shops. All wagon parts were made and assembled on the premises. Completed wagons were raised to the second floor, where they were painted and stored. Before 1910, finished wagons were pulled to the second floor up an outside ramp, but that year an elevator was added to the front of the building to make this step easier.

The Gruber works were powered, first by a water turbine, then by a steam engine, and finally by an Otto (Philadelphia) gasoline engine installed in 1906. Most of the machinery was driven by leather belts connecting the engines to overhead line shafting, as in the interior of the blacksmith shop, opposite.

Also in the blacksmith shop, from left to right, the machines are: a tire-form roller made by Wells Bros. & Co. of Greenfield, Massachusetts; a power press by the Defiance Machine Works, Defiance, Ohio; and a hydraulic tire setter from the West Tire Setter Co., Rochester, New York. In the photograph of the wood shop, below, is a spoke-tennoning machine by the H. B. Smith Machine Company, Smithville, New Jersey in the background, and a spoke-turning lathe by John Gleason of Philadelphia, dated 1873, in the foreground.

Smithfield Street Bridge, Pittsburgh

# Transportation and Communication

*Thy knitted frame, thy springs and valves, the tremu-*
*    lous twinkle of thy wheels,*
*Thy train of cars behind, obedient, merrily following,*
*Through gale or calm, now swift, now slack, yet*
*    steadily careering;*
*Type of the modern—emblem of motion and power*
*    —pulse of the continent . . .*

Like every other American, Walt Whitman, author of these lines in "To a Locomotive in Winter," was in love with journeying, and felt the American fascination with the engines, terminals, bridges and highways that served the traveler. The industries that involve transport seem especially to touch the national character, summing up its restlessness, its desire to be going places and doing things—preferably at a distance and in a hurry. The various transport facilities in the pages that follow all partake in one way or another of the excitement of the journey, and express the everlasting optimism that fulfillment lies at the end of the road.

81

Scale, 96.

SAND KEY.

First Order Lens.

# Sand Key Light

THIS IS THE SECOND oldest of six iron screw-pile lighthouses that were built along this part of the Florida coast in the 1850s to warn shipping away from a string of offshore reefs, shoals and keys. The Sand Key structure was designed by the noted lighthouse engineer J. W. P. Lewis, fabricated by the John P. Riley Ironworks of Charleston, South Carolina, and erected in 1853 under the supervision of Lieutenant George G. Meade, who commanded the Union Army at Gettysburg ten years later.

The Sand Key light's tower is 132 feet high and slopes inward from a base 50 feet square to a 19-foot-square platform supporting the watchroom and lantern enclosure. The lighthouse's foundation is made up of seventeen 8-inch diameter wrought-iron pilings fitted with helicoidal screws (see opposite). The pilings are bored 10 feet into the sand and coral sea bed. On top of the pilings are concrete caps and iron-web spread footings, or bases, 4 feet in diameter. The tower frame is composed of 8-inch cast-iron pipe columns, tied by coupling boxes and braced with 3-inch and 1½-inch wrought-iron tension and compression rods. Connections are made with bolts or hooks and turnbuckles.

The present lighthouse keeper's quarters (built in 1874 to replace the original) are on the lower wood-deck platform in a 30-foot-square cast-iron and sheet-metal box. There are windows, and the sheet-metal panels have ventilator scoops. The quarters are no longer used. The light's machinery is now fully automated and requires only periodic servicing by the United States Coast Guard, which maintains the Sand Key Lighthouse.

The central riveted steel-plate cylinder contains a 7-foot diameter cast-iron spiral stair. At the observation platform above is a watchroom, 12 feet in diameter, and on top of that (with access by ladder) is the lantern-house. This upper section, from the platform top to the lanternhouse dome, is also of cast iron.

Machinery for revolving the light was kept in the watchroom, but now all equipment—including a modern battery-operated light of 16-mile range—is contained within the lanternhouse. An iron ladder from shore level to the first platform was removed some time ago as a precaution against vandalism. Projecting off in a westerly direction is a wood dock and boathouse, supported on iron and wood framing.

# Ferry Building

## SAN FRANCISCO, CALIFORNIA
## 1903

IN ITS HEYDAY, San Francisco's Ferry Building was one of the two busiest transport terminals in the world (the other was Charing Cross Station, London). Fifty million people each year passed by the splendid arches of the Ferry Building's facade. In magnitude the terminal was equal to the vast crowds, extending almost 700 feet along San Francisco's waterfront in the section known as the Embarcadero. Its tower, modeled on the Giralda Tower at Seville, is 240 feet high.

The Ferry Building has been a part of the daily life of San Francisco for seventy-five years. It first signaled the noon hour by an automatically-triggered black ball that slid down a tall pole mounted on the tower. From 1918 well into mid-century, a siren, which replaced the time ball, resounded across San Francisco Bay three times each day. When the weather was right, the siren could be heard in six counties.

The Ferry Building was officially opened in 1898, but it was not fully complete until 1903. It replaced an earlier one-story wood structure built in 1877. The Ferry Building is solidly constructed on a forest of concrete substructure. It was virtually untouched by the 1906 San Francisco Earthquake.

The above-ground structure is steel and brick covered on the outside with a gray Colusa sandstone, and a large portion of the interior was originally covered with marble. The first floor main entrance led inside to ferry-line waiting rooms and the usual assortment of conveniences, including telephone booths, a telegraph office, vendors' stands and baggage rooms.

But the major attraction was the second floor—a two-story steel-arched room running the length of the building (opposite, bottom). Now much altered, but once used for grand civic functions and flower shows, the famous hall displayed a huge relief map of California. The site has, besides the Ferry Building, extensive docks and seawalls, totalling $18\frac{1}{2}$ miles of berthing space for international shipping.

During World War II, the Navy occupied the Ferry Building, except for one section used by the Southern Pacific Railroad to carry its passengers from Oakland to San Francisco. East Bay commuter service had ended by 1939. After the War, the new Bay bridges made even the Southern Pacific's ferries obsolete. Their last ferry made its final trip across the Bay in 1958.

The Ferry Building was renovated in 1956, and now houses state offices and a World Trade Center. The new Bay Area Rapid Transit subway-train tube runs under the building's south wing (right-hand side in the top photo).

85

# Delaware Aqueduct

## LACKAWAXEN, PENNSYLVANIA TO MINISINK, NEW YORK

### 1847–8

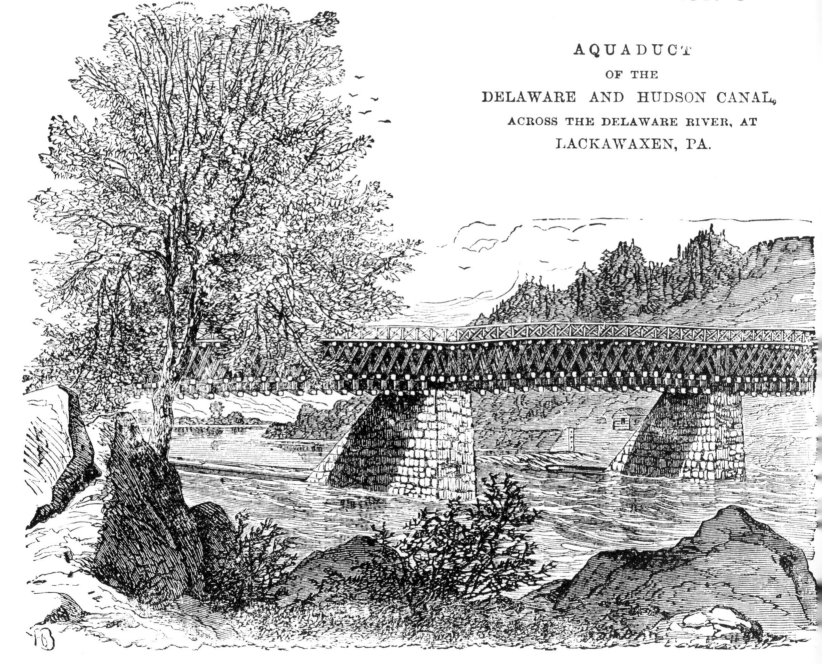

AQUADUCT

OF THE

DELAWARE AND HUDSON CANAL,

ACROSS THE DELAWARE RIVER, AT

LACKAWAXEN, PA.

THE DELAWARE AND HUDSON CANAL opened in 1829 as the principal waterway that tied northeastern Pennsylvania's anthracite coal fields to domestic and industrial consumers in New York. Its 108-mile length began at Honesdale, Pennsylvania and ran roughly east to Port Jervis, New York, where it turned sharply to the northeast, continuing to Rondout, New York, near Kingston, where it entered the Hudson. Canal traffic was basically one-way, consisting of barges carrying coal from west to east.

The canal system had to be made ever more efficient to remain competitive with the rapidly developing railroads. Increased efficiency was secured up to the 1870s by larger and larger coal barges, and by improvements to the waterway itself, including construction of the Delaware Aqueduct.

This was a water-carrying bridge spanning the Delaware River in northeastern Pennsylvania at the New York border. Apparently the oldest suspension bridge in the United States, the aqueduct was designed and built by John Roebling. It is the earliest remaining example of Roebling's engineering genius, and it presages

Contemporary engineer's rough sketch of aqueduct, dated 27 February 1847

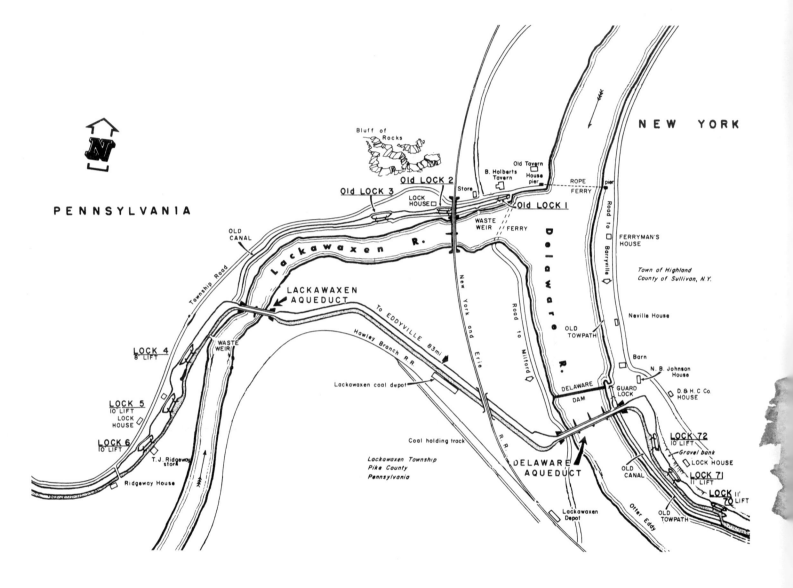

his masterpiece, the Brooklyn Bridge.

The aqueduct was built to facilitate the movement of boats through the Delaware–Hudson canal. The Canal had originally been laid out so that barges entered the Delaware through a lock on the north bank of the Lackawaxen River, where it joined the larger river. The barges were then floated, or hand-hauled by a rope ferry, to the eastern bank of the Delaware, where they rejoined the canal. This passage of the Delaware was an awkward

88

operation that frequently resulted in bottlenecks.

In the high-water months of fall and spring, furthermore, the crossing was sometimes impossible, and traffic came to a standstill. The situation was further complicated by the large numbers of timber rafts that came down the Delaware, creating vast confusion when they encountered coal barges trying to cross the stream.

The Delaware Aqueduct, located downstream from the old rope ferry (see map above), solved the cross-

ing problem handsomely—for about thirty years. In time, the Canal lost out to the railroads. The Delaware–Hudson waterway declined from the mid-1870s on, and finally sold off its property in 1899. The aqueduct was bought by a private owner and converted into a highway bridge (page 89). This was done fairly easily. Towpaths were sawed off, a pedestrian walk was built on the downstream side of the aqueduct's floor, and a tollhouse was added on the New York end.

In the early 1930s, following damage by fire, the wood portions of the old aqueduct were stripped away, revealing the structural cables as we see them today (opposite), and the present wood floor was installed. The aqueduct is still maintained as a tollbridge.

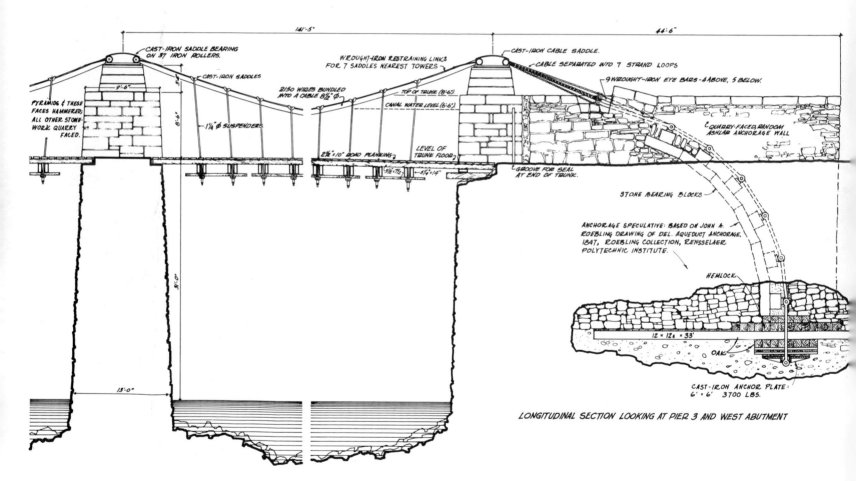

LONGITUDINAL SECTION LOOKING AT PIER 3 AND WEST ABUTMENT

90

91

# Starrucca Viaduct

STARRUCCA VIADUCT'S simplicity, and its great size, make it one of the most impressive monuments in American industrial archeology. It was built at the same time as the Delaware Aqueduct, and is located about fifty miles northwest of it.

The viaduct is built of locally-quarried gray sandstone, and is composed of 17 arches in 51-foot spans. It is 1,040 feet long, 25 feet wide at the top, and approximately 100 feet high. The viaduct was the largest bridge on what was, in its time, the longest railroad in the world—the 445-mile New York and Erie line.

Starrucca Viaduct linked the railroad's roadbed on either side of the Starrucca Creek valley in as straight and level a way as was possible, so locomotives did not have to climb or descend the steep valley slopes. The railroad might have chosen to lay a gradually-descending roadbed into and across the valley itself. It elected to throw a viaduct over the valley because that was the quickest way across, and the railroad stood to lose its charter if it was not in operation from Piermont, north of New York City, to Binghamton by the end of 1848.

Construction on the viaduct began in the spring of 1847 and was finished by the autumn of 1848, at a cost of about $335,000. Wood derricks were used to hoist the stones into place. An unusual feature at the time were the concrete foundations under the thirteen central, full-height stone piers. These foundations are an early instance of the rediscovery of concrete, a building material well known to the ancient Romans.

The first locomotive traveled the Starrucca span on December 9, 1848. Originally the viaduct carried a single broad-gauge track. Later a second track was

added, and in the 1880s both were replaced by two standard-gauge tracks. These changes were easily made because of the structure's generous width. The viaduct has been repaired from time to time, and trains of considerably higher tonnage than those it was designed to carry still cross it regularly.

Starrucca Viaduct almost certainly was designed by Julius W. Adams, superintending engineer for the New York and Erie Railroad's central division. Its construction was supervised mainly by Adams's brother-in-law, the distinguished engineer James J. Kirkwood.

93

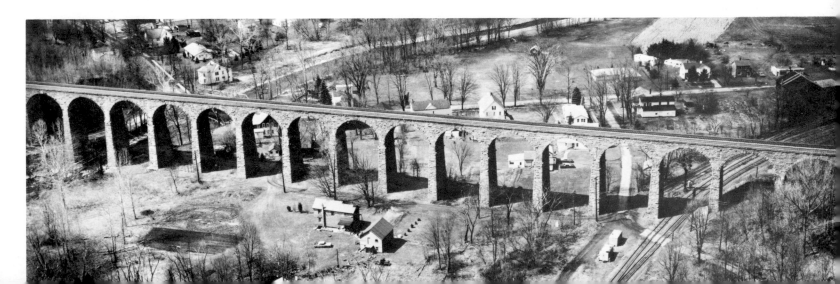

# Bridges

DELAWARE AQUEDUCT and Starrucca Viaduct are two of America's great solutions to the problem of crossing a river or valley. Spanning obstacles has always been a challenge, and the ways in which engineers have accepted that challenge in different times and places are always interesting. There are literally hundreds of bridge designs, in wood, masonry, iron, steel, and concrete. Here are a few of them:

THE UNION COVERED BRIDGE in Monroe County, Missouri, is an example of Theodore Burr's wood arch truss, patented in 1817, which enjoyed great popularity in the nineteenth century. By combining the principles of the diagonally-braced rectangular frame or truss with the arch (see interior, below), Burr was being somewhat cautious. As Ithiel Towne demonstrated with his lattice truss, wood trusses of reasonable span could stand alone.

Roof and siding protected the roadway and the bridge's structure from the elements. The exterior view shows the siding carried down at the ends of the bridge to cover the arches' sides.

THE BOLLMAN SUSPENSION AND TRUSSED BRIDGE over the Little Patuxent River at Savage, Maryland (opposite), is the last of its kind. It was built in 1869 and relocated to the present site in 1888. The Baltimore & Ohio Railroad built a number of these

bridges in the mid-nineteenth century, but they were eventually superseded by other types of metal bridges that used less material.

Structurally, the Bollman bridge looks like a rectangular truss with diagonal bracing superimposed. In fact, the bridge is a series of trussed beams. The verticals and horizontals are cast iron. The tension bars that radiate out from end and center piers to the bases of each vertical are wrought iron.

All the parts are pinned together, a quick and easy way of assembling prefabricated components. The break in the center (below) was for the sake of economy, it being cheaper to make two short spans than a single long one.

95

# Bridges

LIKE OTHERS of its type, this iron through-truss bridge, located about six miles north of Provo, Utah, suggests the construction of a boy's erector set. The span has a complicated past, for it contains parts from an 1884 bridge made by the Union Bridge Company of Buffalo, New York, and erected by the narrow-gauge DENVER & RIO GRANDE WESTERN RAILROAD at Green River, Utah.

In 1900, when the line converted to standard-gauge track, the bridge was replaced. It was then reduced from about 165 feet to its present 82-foot length, modified for standard-gauge equipment, and relocated over the Price River near Wellington, Utah. In 1919, the bridge was moved again, to its present site on the D&RGWRR's "Heber Creeper" line, which ran 32 miles from Provo to Heber. Trains still cross the bridge occasionally.

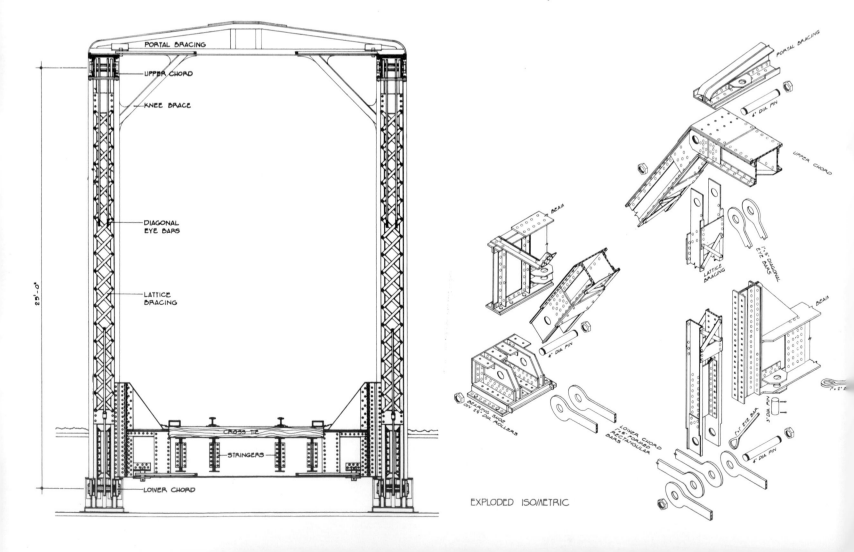

EXPLODED ISOMETRIC

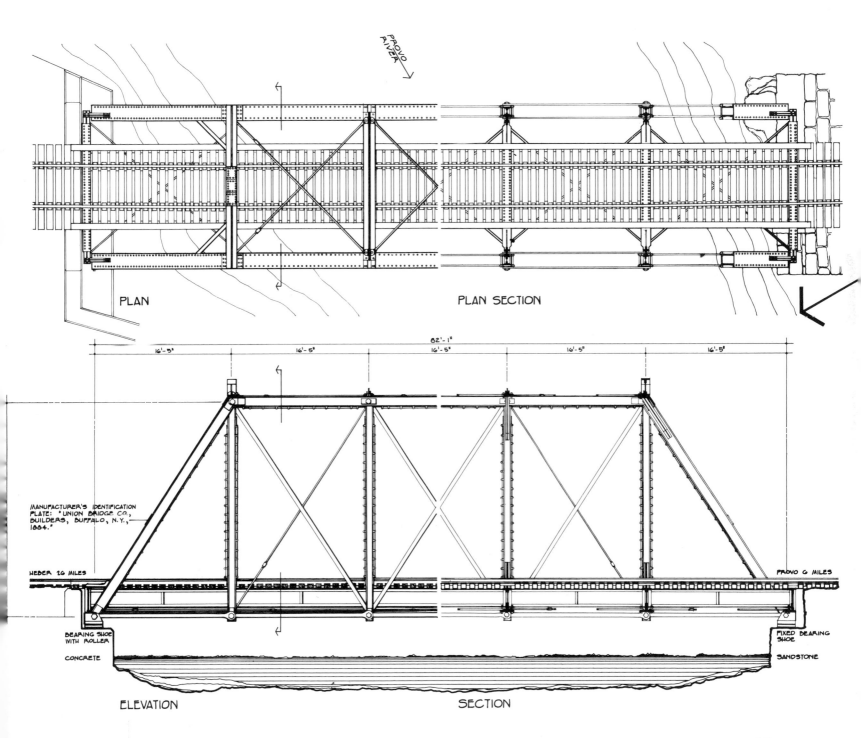

PROVO
RIVER

PLAN

PLAN SECTION

82'-1"

16'-5" 16'-5" 16'-5" 16'-5" 16'-5"

MANUFACTURER'S IDENTIFICATION
PLATE: "UNION BRIDGE CO.,
BUILDERS, BUFFALO, N.Y.,
1884."

HEBER 26 MILES

PROVO 6 MILES

BEARING SHOE
WITH ROLLER

FIXED BEARING
SHOE

CONCRETE

SANDSTONE

ELEVATION

SECTION

97

THE OGDEN–LUCIN CUT-OFF Trestle seems to race across Utah's shallow Great Salt Lake. It was designed and built by the Southern Pacific Railroad's chief engineer, William Hood, as part of a new line connecting Ogden on the east to Lucin, west of the lake.

The need for the trestle was similar to the need for the Starrucca Viaduct—a level roadbed. The Ogden–Lucin span replaced an earlier section of the Southern Pacific line that ran north through the Promontory Mountains. By eliminating the mountain line, the bridge by-passed some 43 miles of extreme grades and hazardous curves.

The project was begun in March 1902, and was completed in mid-November 1903 at a cost of roughly $5 million. The permanent trestle, a segment of which is shown in the drawing, is approximately 11 miles long, which must make it one of the largest wood structures in the world. Though it is still in use, the trestle today is secondary to a parallel causeway the railroad built in the late 1950s.

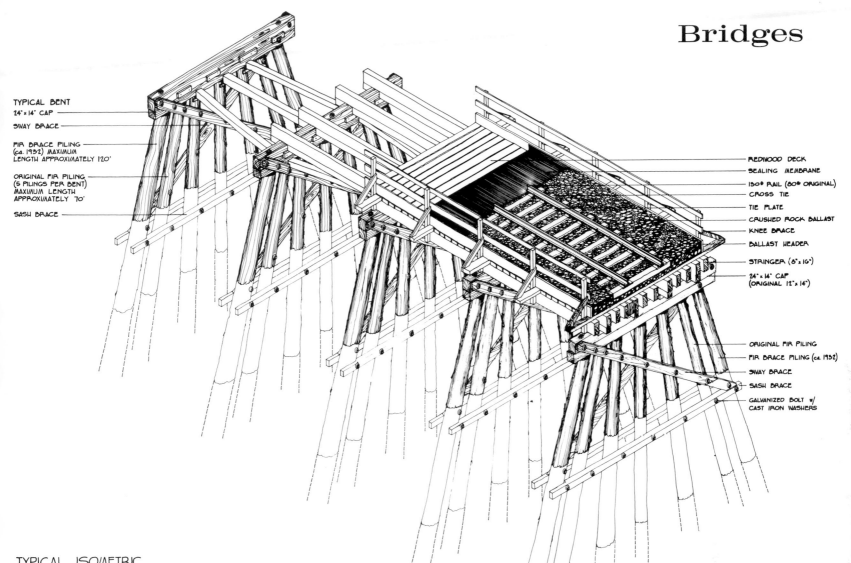

TYPICAL BENT
24" x 14" CAP
SWAY BRACE

FIR BRACE PILING
(ca. 1932) MAXIMUM
LENGTH APPROXIMATELY 120'

ORIGINAL FIR PILING
(5 PILINGS PER BENT)
MAXIMUM LENGTH
APPROXIMATELY 70'

SASH BRACE

REDWOOD DECK
SEALING MEMBRANE
130# RAIL (80# ORIGINAL)
CROSS TIE
TIE PLATE
CRUSHED ROCK BALLAST
KNEE BRACE
BALLAST HEADER
STRINGER (8" x 16")
24" x 14" CAP
(ORIGINAL 12" x 14")

ORIGINAL FIR PILING
FIR BRACE PILING (ca. 1932)
SWAY BRACE
SASH BRACE
GALVANIZED BOLT w/
CAST IRON WASHERS

TYPICAL ISOMETRIC

# Bridges

THE TUNKHANNOCK VIADUCT was built between 1912 and 1915 by the Lackawanna Railroad to
improve its road between Scranton, Pennsylvania and
Binghamton, New York. It is the largest concrete bridge
in America, nearly half a mile long, and rising 240 feet
above the bed of Tunkhannock Creek near Nicholson,

Pennsylvania. The span carries two tracks over its ten
arches. The Tunkhannock Viaduct was one of the last
of its kind to be built. By the time of its completion, the
heyday of the great railroads had passed, and the wealth
required for monumental bridges in concrete, like the
Tunkhannock, was no longer available.

100

The big concrete state highway bridge over the Susquehanna at CLARK'S FERRY, near Harrisburg, Pennsylvania, is the fifth bridge to cross the river there. The first bridge on the site, built in 1828–9, was part of the Pennsylvania Canal, which ran from Philadelphia to Pittsburgh. The present bridge was built in 1925 by a private tollbridge company.

In the pictures on these pages, note that both the Tunkhannock and Clark's Ferry bridges have open-spandrel arches, a feature that decreased weight and wind resistance.

# Bridges

This three-span structure at FORT LARAMIE, Wyoming, believed to be the oldest military bridge west of the Mississippi, looks like a series of arches, but really is made up of individual bow-string trusses, a type of span design that was used by many of the earliest American metal bridges. The system of vertical, diagonal and horizontal members combines with the arch to make each of the three spans a fully stable, self-contained structure. The spreading forces at the ends of the arch are held in check by tension in the horizontal members. In effect, then, the bridge is three separate bridges placed end to end. Its date is given on a stone marker as 1875, but a plate gives the manufacturer and the date July 3, 1867, almost certainly the patent date.

# Starrucca House

**SUSQUEHANNA, PENNSYLVANIA    ca. 1865**

NOW DESERTED, this great sad-faced brick building still conveys a suggestion of its original grandeur. It is a railroad station hotel, the last significant one of its kind remaining.

Station hotels were important focal points in the history of American passenger rail service from just before the Civil War until about 1880, when they were superseded by sleeping and dining cars. In the days when Susquehanna was a busy stop on the Erie Railroad, the Starrucca House was one of the region's chief attractions.

The hotel's Gothic Revival design closely resembles a sketch submitted by the architect E. J. M. Derrick. Originally there were twin cupolas near the center where the two gables meet the main roof. There was a continu-

ous one-story canopy, too, along the entire 300-foot length of the building facing the tracks.

Inside, the Starrucca House was divided into three parts, the center portion housing a huge dining hall the full height of the structure. Hotel rooms, waiting rooms, ticket offices and other railroad facilities were in the two-story portions on either side.

The Starrucca House closed in 1903, and the building later was converted to railroad offices and a railroad YMCA. The dining room was subdivided into three floors to contain a gymnasium and sleeping quarters for 135 men. Unoccupied since the late 1960s, the building has come close to destruction, and recent plans for its conversion to new uses have not yet been put into effect.

# Union Station

THE LOUISVILLE & NASHVILLE Railroad built the Union Station complex at Montgomery in a major project that included passenger and freight stations and a train shed. The plan of the passenger station called for a "one-sided" building to fill the narrow space that was available; the station, which is 315 feet long, is only 44 feet deep. Behind its subdued Romanesque facade, the building contains waiting rooms, ticket offices, a dining room and kitchens. Stonework is of granite, with decorative brickwork and black marble. The station is timber-framed.

Montgomery's Union Station was part of an extensive building campaign undertaken by the Louisville & Nashville in the 1890s. Stations and other buildings were also

built in Louisville and in Nashville, though the Montgomery project was apparently the most extensive of the three.

The waiting room, seen at right above, was quite opulent. Note especially the patterned tile floors, wainscoting and ornamental glass in the windows over the entrance.

The Louisville & Nashville's train shed at Montgomery is one of eleven such structures that still survive in the U.S. It is more interesting architecturally than the grander station. The train shed is 600 feet long and spans 79 feet. Although lacking the elaborate decorations of the other structures on the site, it is just as impressive in its functional simplicity as the more ornate buildings.

104

These pages show the train shed in detail. Especially noteworthy is the wood-and-iron construction of the roof, in which a pair of trussed beams are connected by a network of ties (the detail of the tying members at left shows that the roof employed a rich variety of iron compressive struts and tension rods or bars).

Van Buren and Dearborn Streets

Wabash Avenue at Lake Street

# Union Loop

CHICAGO, ILLINOIS 1897

THE UNION LOOP, a massive web of riveted steel girders and shining tracks, arches over busy city streets, passing close by the windows of tall buildings on either side, and insistently threads its way through down-town Chicago.

Rapid transit came to Chicago in 1892 in the form of an elevated railway with bi-directional steam engines pulling open-platform wood coaches made by the Gilbert

109

Crossover, Lake and Wells Streets

Car Company of Green Island, New York. In 1895 electric motor cars and trailers were introduced.

The downtown segment of the elevated system, called the Loop, was built to provide a circuit of Chicago's central business district. It was used in common by the

equipment of four private rapid transit companies. Initially traffic was two-way; from 1913 to 1969 it was one-way; and now once again it has become two-way. Various extensions, additions and mergers have occurred in the intervening years, and in 1947 the entire system came

Station, Randolph Street at Wabash Avenue

under control of the Chicago Transit Authority.

For the industrial archeologist, the Chicago Loop provides an ideal case study of an entire transit system of reasonably manageable size that still serves its original purpose. The elevated structures and commuter stations still remain in relatively good condition. The stations, like the one at Quincy Street (page 115), are excellent examples of metallic architecture in the exuberant classical style made fashionable by Chicago's World's Columbian Exposition of 1893.

Lake and Wells Streets

114

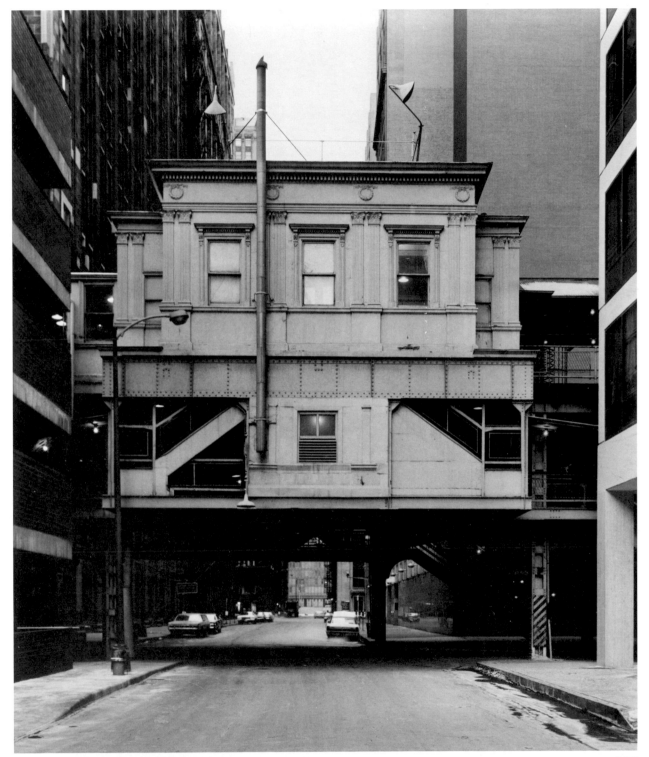

Station, Quincy Street at Wells Street

Conveyor, coke works, West Virginia

# The Practice of Industrial Archeology

MODERN INDUSTRIAL HISTORY began in Western Europe around 1700—the opening of the so-called "Industrial Revolution." Most industrial archeologists are concerned with sites and structures dating from this time or later. Of course, older remains, going all the way back to prehistory, could be considered as well, but survivals from before the industrial revolution commonly fall within the scope of prehistoric, classical or medieval archeology or the general history of technology.

The modern period that industrial archeology has made its own is rich in material for study because of its very proximity to us. We have a great deal of information, and attempting to understand it is a complicated task. No one individual can fully master all the skills required. Collaboration is essential, and thus industrial archeology stresses multi-disciplinary co-operation. We can see this in R. A. Buchanan's definition of industrial archeology, which we cited at the beginning of this book. By that definition, industrial archeology is composed of four activities: investigating, surveying, recording, and preserving.

The first of these, investigating, involves searching for information about an industrial site and exploring for its precise location. Industrial archeologists usually, but not always, start with some knowledge both of a site's importance and of its location. There are occasions, however, when written accounts tell about an industrial activity in a region, though surface remains have disappeared. In other cases, the student stumbles upon ruins of an old industrial site about which nothing much is known. What does one do in these cases?

In the first instance, one reads accounts closely for clues to the vanished industry's exact location, checks maps and old views of the locale, and talks with "old timers" who might be able to shed some light. Perhaps they or a relative worked there. Or they may recall playing among the ruins as children. There's no single best approach; one tries to pinpoint the location as exactly as one can, and then explores the terrain with a sharp eye, taking care not to unduly disturb potentially valuable evidence.

In the opposite situation, where a site is found about which little is known, the same kinds of sources are consulted, with the aim of finding hints about what was made there, what processes were used, and how the site might fit into the overall development of an industry or region. It's also possible that records or other papers have survived that bear directly on the site, so be prepared to poke into dusty attics and leaf through soiled account books. Don't discount anything as a possible lead. It doesn't take much imagination to recognize the value of local libraries and historical societies; but don't forget newspapers, insurance records and even picture postcards.

Interviews are an extremely good source of information as well, if they can be obtained. The people who lived and worked in an industrial community are vital links to the past; they can aid substantially in reconstructing what it was like to work in a factory and in discovering how things were made there. These recollections cannot always be relied on for strict factual accuracy, but they may provide invaluable glimpses into industrial life that no set of statistics could ever yield.

Since most industrial archeologists are concerned with sites less than three hundred years old, structures are frequently still intact or largely so. And even if a building no longer stands whole, portions may be incorporated into later construction, or there may be sufficiently extensive ruins of walls, waterpower canals and out-buildings to permit fairly accurate graphic reconstruction. Investigating the site may also mean looking for such clues as industrial waste heaps, transportation lines and simple repetitive dwellings, which could have been mill workers' houses.

A word of caution. The most vulnerable kind of on-site evidence is the discarded artifact. Old tools, and fragments

117

of machinery or structure and other débris commonly associated with abandoned industry give valuable insights into what was at a site and the way products were made. There is, unfortunately, an almost irresistible temptation to take these as souvenirs. This, as much as the inevitable vandalism, just makes the industrial archeologist's job more difficult. Leave relics in place, unless a truly valuable object is in question. In this case, the artifact should be taken to a safe place (a museum, not your home), after careful field notes of its exact location have been made. If you are unsure of the value of an item you have found, get an expert's opinion. This can be done quickly through the Society for Industrial Archeology, about which more later.

Surveying, the second facet of industrial archeology, assumes that an industrial site has been located, investigated, and found to be interesting. In the survey, the site is described as precisely and completely as possible. Surveying techniques vary according to what has survived at a site. If a complete building survives, it should be accurately measured and thoroughly photographed inside and out. If there are no above-ground remains, excavation may be necessary. Both measurement and excavation require training, but the latter requires special skills and definitely should not be undertaken by amateurs. A badly conducted dig will just confuse matters, and quite possibly destroy the very evidence one is seeking. For surveyors of industrial structures that still remain, or whose ruins are extensive, the proper methods of field measuring, notation and survey photography are not hard to learn.

Recording, the third activity, includes both preparation of final written and graphic survey summaries, and making sure these are either published or placed where others may have access to them. At the very least, copies should be filed with the state historic preservation office and with the Historic American Engineering Record in Washington, D.C. If a site you are interested in is of more than usual significance, consult your state historic preservation officer about applying for a listing in the U.S. Department of the Interior's National Register of Historic Places. Publishing opportunities for survey data range from local or state mimeographed reports to articles in scholarly journals.

A very good guide for beginners in both surveying and recording is Harley J. McKee's *Recording Historic Buildings* (see bibliography). The National Park Service's Historic American Building Survey has occasionally recorded industrial buildings since its founding in the 1930s. Its sister agency, the Historic American Engineering Record (HAER), formed in 1969, and mentioned a moment ago, has now taken on the job full time. The HAER's goal is a complete nationwide inventory of important engineering and industrial sites, prepared on a state-by-state basis. The large-scale HAER program requires co-operation and initiative from the public as well as from professionals in the field. HAER personnel, as well as friends of industrial archeology in localities all over the U.S., continue to compile detailed data on sites of every possible description for the HAER inventory. If you think you know of an important industrial site, let HAER know. If it is an unusual site, HAER may even be able to arrange for a summer field recording team to actually do the surveying and recording work.

Industrial archeology's fourth component is preservation. There are several approaches to preserving industrial sites. The first and most obvious is "historic preservation," which consists in saving rare and highly significant industrial structures and sites, places that are unique, or that witnessed important achievements in American industrial history. The essential purpose of these sites is to serve as the very best representatives of our rich industrial past. Some even lend themselves to becoming working museums where one can see older industrial processes actually being carried on. In evaluating any site that may merit historic preservation, a rigorous set of standards must be applied, standards that will insure we signify only what is truly historic. Indiscriminate classification, no matter how well-intentioned, insidiously leads to undervaluing historically important places. Certainly all industrial sites should be investigated, surveyed, and recorded. But historic preservation should be limited to unique and outstanding examples.

One further word on this category. Monuments worthy of historic preservation need not be isolated buildings or single-structure sites. Recent emphasis on preserving regions or districts, rather than single buildings, implies an approach we may call "comprehensive preservation." In this approach, the object is to set aside whole enclaves that represent types of economic organization: farm settlements, mill villages, residential neighborhoods, market areas and industrial complexes.

There are also other ways we can save perfectly sound, but historically unimportant, old industrial structures. This second approach to preservation is adaptive use. Old industrial buildings are frequently well built, and often have large open interior spaces that can be easily converted for new purposes. Many obsolete factory buildings have great potential for totally new uses. They are, in fact, a national resource we have neglected for far too long. But there are more and more instances of re-use, and there are several spectacular conversions that have already been done, including San Francisco's Ghirardelli Square, where a chocolate factory has been turned into shops and restaurants, and

Boston's Chickering Piano Factory, now craft-guild, artist-in-residence housing. Both show how industrial structures can be handsomely and economically transformed, and in the process kept as living parts of our environment.

Industrial preservation, then, may range from the highest and most selective historic preservation on either a district-wide or individual-site basis, to the equally important conserving of what we already possess in high-quality structures through re-use of older industrial buildings.

All four activities included in our definition of industrial archeology—investigating, surveying, recording, and preserving industrial sites—are encouraged by the Society for Industrial Archeology (SIA). Formed in 1971, the Society has grown steadily in membership, and currently has nearly a thousand members. The majority are in the United States and Canada, but there are members from as far away as Australia. The SIA publishes a popular newsletter six times a year, as well as *IA*, a semi-annual journal containing scholarly articles, field reports and book reviews. The SIA holds an annual conference at a different location each year to draw attention to historically important industrial sites. The Society also sponsors occasional regional field trips.

Readers who would like more information about SIA should write to:

The Society for Industrial Archeology
Room 5020
National Museum of History and Technology
Smithsonian Institution
Washington, D.C. 20560

Interior, Louisville Water Company Pumping Station

# A Note on UTM Map Co-Ordinates

The Universal Transverse Mercator (UTM) map co-ordinate system is useful in industrial archeological research because it provides an easy way of precisely locating sites. On maps that employ the UTM grid—including all modern 7.5- and 15-minute U.S. Geological Survey (USGS) quadrangle maps—the system permits sites to be pinpointed to within 100 meters (300 feet), which is usually precise enough to enable map readers to locate existing structures.

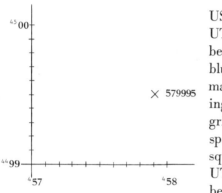

On the widely used USGS quadrangle maps, UTM co-ordinate numbers are indicated by blue "tick" marks in the map margins. Connecting these ticks creates a grid network of evenly spaced 1 kilometer squares. On the maps, UTM grid ticks are numbered with small superscript numbers and larger main numbers (*e.g.*, ⁴⁴99 in the example). The small superscript digits refer to larger map divisions within which the local map is included, and may be ignored in determining co-ordinates of a given point within a specific maps area, since the larger area within which the point lies is usually identified simply by the name of the USGS quadrangle map itself. This is the method used in the list of UTM co-ordinates below, for the sites in this book.

Specific points on a map are defined in six-digit co-ordinates: three digits taken from the horizontal map margin (read first) and three from the vertical margin. To produce a six-digit co-ordinate number for the point 579995 in the example, find the first two digits (5 and 7) on the horizontal margin, and the fourth and fifth digits (9 and 9) on the vertical margin. Count tenths of a kilometer from the horizontal and vertical grid lines to supply the third and sixth digits (9 and 5), locating the precise point you want.

Although six-digit UTM co-ordinates are adequate for most purposes, expanded co-ordinates employing up to fifteen digits are sometimes used to facilitate computer storage of data. Expanded co-ordinates are used for many of the sites on the list of American industrial sites, Appendix IV. For more information about the use of these fuller co-ordinates and about the UTM system generally, write the Society for Industrial Archeology, Room 5020, National Museum of History & Technology, Washington, D.C. 20560.

# Co-Ordinates for Selected Sites

Following are UTM grid co-ordinates for forty-four of the sites described in the text. In all cases place-names refer to the named quadrangles used in the U.S. Geological Survey maps.

*Silver King Ore Loading Station:* Park City East (Utah) 579995.

*Sumpter Valley Gold Dredge:* Canyon City (1:250,000 scale map) (Oregon) 047547.

*Oil Rig:* Petroleum (West Virginia) 762431.

*Mercury Coal & Coke Co.:* Masontown (West Virginia) 020778.

*Elkins Coal & Coke Co.:* Morgantown South (West Virginia) 942846.

*Cascade Ovens:* Masontown (West Virginia) 020795.

*Richard Ovens:* Morgantown South (West Virginia) 942846.

*Tintic Standard Reduction Mill:* Santaquin (Utah) 271234.

*Sloss Blast Furnaces:* Birmingham North (Alabama) 193088.

*Mercur Ghost Town:* Mercur (Utah) 977640.

*Grain Elevator, Texhoma:* Stevens NE (Texas) 500420 (approximate).

*Grain Elevator, Cresbard:* Cresbard (South Dakota) 041012 (approximate).

*Grain Elevator, Everett:* Everett (Texas) 428012.

*American (Wiessner) Brewery:* Baltimore East   631521.

*Tivoli Brewery:* Fort Logan (Colorado)   995992.

*Harrisville:* Monadnock (New Hampshire) 370586.

*Pejepscot (Topsham) Paper Mill:* Bath (Maine)   225634.

*Eclipse Windmill:* Sheffield NW (Texas)   153050.

*Bronson Windmill:* Westport (Connecticut)   432591.

*Shepherd's Gristmill:* Shepherdstown (West Virginia)   588684.

*Buffalo Bill Dam:* Cody (Wyoming)   444289.

*Mountain Dell Dam:* Mountain Dell (Utah)   392111.

*Adams Power Plant:* Niagara Falls (New York)   593715.

*Water Company Pumping Station:* Jeffersonville (Kentucky)   135375.

*Gasholder House:* Troy South (New York)   072305.

*Robbins & Lawrence Machine Shops:* Claremont (New Hampshire)   111166.

*Colt's Armory:* Hartford North (Connecticut)   942251.

*Gruber Wagon Works:* Bernville (Pennsylvania)   101726.

*Rogers Locomotive Shop:* Paterson (New Jersey)   691292.

*Pratt & Whitney Test House:* Hartford South (Connecticut)   969243.

*Sand Key Light:* Key West (1:250,000 scale map)   111044.

*Ferry Building:* San Francisco North   535831.

*Delaware Aqueduct:* Shohola (Pennsylvania–New York)   012921.

*Starrucca Viaduct:* Susquehanna (Pennsylvania)   516457.

*Union Covered Bridge:* Paris West (Missouri)   772649.

*Ogden-Lucin Cut-Off Trestle:* Carrington Island NE (Utah)   719637.

*Bollman Suspension Bridge:* Savage (Maryland)   422331.

*D&RGWRR Truss Bridge:* Bridal Veil Falls (Utah)   444627.

*Bow-String Truss Bridge:* Fort Laramie (Wyoming)   385730.

*Tunkhannock Viaduct:* Factoryville (Pennsylvania)   352080.

*Clark's Ferry Bridge:* Duncannon (Pennsylvania)   295738.

*Starrucca House:* Susquehanna (Pennsylvania)   494435.

*Union Station:* Montgomery North (Alabama)   645826.

*Union Loop (e.g., Quincy Street Station):* Chicago Loop   474362.

Beehive charcoal kilns, Wyoming

## APPENDIX IV

# Selected American Industrial Sites

Industrial remains in the United States are everywhere; we know only a fraction of the sites that exist. The Historic American Engineering Record (HAER), an agency of the National Park Service charged with surveying America's industrial remains, has—as this book goes to press—about 5,000 sites on file. HAER's file grows daily from contributions by staff members, architecture and engineering historians, teachers and students, preservationists and interested members of the public.

Listed here are about 360 places in addition to the 46 whose descriptions comprise the main body of this book. The list is intended to illustrate the wealth and range of industrial remains available in the fifty states, and to guide interested readers to specific sites in their areas. In compiling the list I have tried to show that every part of the country has noteworthy industrial monuments. The HAER files, however, from which most of the material for the sites list comes, can at present only be considered strong in certain northeastern states, and in North Carolina, Colorado, Utah and California. Several states are represented on the list by only one or two sites, and one state, Montana, is not represented at all. Obviously, much work remains to be done.

I want to emphasize that this list is not offered as a selection of the "best" American industrial sites (though many outstanding structures are here). Nor is it in any sense an exhaustive list. There are, for example, some 1,500 covered bridges still standing in the United States, and there are hundreds of iron furnaces; only a few of these appear here, and some industries are not represented at all.

The condition of the sites listed varies widely. Some are going concerns still. Some are ruins—or nearly so—and others, since the time of their recording by HAER, may have become ruins, through fire, vandalism, or the action of the elements.

Readers are urged to visit the places listed for their areas, but in many cases it is necessary to plan visits carefully. I have tried to select sites that are accessible, bearing in mind that what is accessible to the hardy may not seem so to others. Some are in remote locations, however, and some of the buildings are deteriorated. In both cases, prospective visitors are advised to take care: old and decrepit buildings, especially, may be hazardous to enter and explore.

Some of the sites on the list are normally off limits to the public, and others are on private property. Arrangements can often be made to visit the sites in question, but in any case, it is important, as a matter of common courtesy, that would-be visitors get permission to visit all sites not obviously open to the public.

Those who are inspired to explore their areas for industrial remains should keep in mind the very real contribution to American industrial archeology they are in a position to make. If you find a place that you think may not be known, and that you believe should be added to the inventory of American industrial sites, contact HAER (care of National Park Service, Washington, D.C., 20040) and request blank HAER Inventory cards like the one reproduced opposite. These cards are less difficult to complete than may at first appear. Return the card, completed with specifics about your site, to HAER. You will have advanced by a further step a laudable effort to record a fascinating aspect of our national heritage.

### ALABAMA

**Tannehill Furnace**
Bessemer vicinity
Two furnaces, built in 1859 and 1863, survive from an iron works, dating back to 1829, that produced ordnance for the Confederacy until it was razed by Northern forces in 1865.

**Sand Island Light**
Mobile Bay
Ft. Morgan vicinity
  (UTM: 16.398860.3339860)
The lighthouse tower, of masonry, is 132 feet high, and is seated on a timber-and-piling foundation. It was built in 1873.

**Redstone Test Stand**
Dodd Road at Redstone Arsenal
Huntsville (UTM: 16.530560.3832160)
The site includes an iron-frame tower, concrete base, and blockhouses used until 1961 for testing Redstone ballistic missiles, and

for launching early U.S. space vehicles. Access to the site is restricted.

**Gulf, Mobile & Ohio RR Station**
Beauregard and St. Joseph Streets
Mobile (UTM: 16.399860.3396660)
The massive station, in the Spanish Colonial Revival style, is a domed building with an arcaded front and baroque elements. It was built in 1907.

**Magnolia Warehouse**
62 Lipscomb Street
Mobile
A handsome survivor of the once-common waterfront warehouses that stored the Old South's abundant cotton. The warehouse dates from ca. 1866.

**Boshell's Mill**
Cedrum
Townley vicinity
The site includes a small sandstone dam and two buildings operated as grist- and saw-

mills in the 1890s; milling apparatus is intact. Access to the site is restricted.

### ALASKA

**Steamer** *Nenana*
  Alaskaland
  Fairbanks
*Nenana* is the best surviving example of the old stern-wheel steam packet boats that carried passengers and freight on the Yukon River. Built in 1933, she ran until 1955, and has been converted into a restaurant and club.

**Hope Mining Village**
Hope Road
Hope
Placer gold mining thrived at Hope from 1896 to 1910; the last extensive mining operation ceased in the early 1940s. The condition of remaining buildings varies from excellent to ruined.

## HAER INVENTORY

| 1. NAME OF STRUCTURE | 2. DATE | 3. NATURE OF STRUCTURE | 4. INDUSTRIAL CLASSIFICATION |
|---|---|---|---|
| American Brewery (formerly Wiessner's) | ·1887 | | BULK: FOOD: BEVG. (13.2)  PS&PM:STEAM:COR.(40.0) |

| 5. LOCATION: STREET & NUMBER | CITY OR TOWN | COUNTY | STATE | 6. USGS QUAD MAP & UTM GRID REF. |
|---|---|---|---|---|
| 1701 North Gay Street | Baltimore | BALTIMORE CITY (510) | MD | BALTIMORE EAST  18.363120.4352110 |

OWNER OF PROPERTY    ADDRESS
Allegheny Brewery Corp., 2216 N. Charles Street, Baltimore, Md.

7. CONDITION: □ EXCELLENT □ GOOD □ FAIR □ DETERIORATED □ RUINS □ UNEXPOSED □ ALTERED □ ACCESSIBLE TO PUBLIC

9. DESCRIPTION & BACKGROUND HISTORY: NUMBER OF STRUCTURES; DIMENSIONS; FABRIC; STRUCTURE & FORM; SURVIVING MACHINERY, FITTINGS AND EQUIPMENT; APPROX. AREA OF SITE; ALTERATIONS; PRESENT USE; ENGINEER; ARCHITECT; DESIGNER; IMPORTANT EVENTS & INDIVIDUALS.

The American Brewery ceased operations on March 30, 1973, leaving in jeopardy one of the finest "Teutonic Breweryesque" style breweries in the country. Originally established by John F. Wiessner in 1863, the present structure was built to enlarge and modernize the operations. With prohibition, the brewery failed and was sold to the FitzSimmons family, owners of the American Malt Co., subsequently American Brewery. As important as the structure itself is the refrigeration equipment consisting of: 3 steam-driven ammonia compressors, one of which was built in 1884 by Fred Wolf, Chicago, and probably is the oldest American refrigeration engine extant. The steam cylinder is by Gebruder Wintertheur. The engine has been donated to the Smithsonian. Across the street are related buildings: a residence for the owners (1896) and offices built in three periods -- 1892, 1896, and 1900.

10. PHOTOGRAPHS & SKETCH MAP ON REVERSE SIDE.

11. RELATED SOURCES OF INFORMATION: HISTORICAL REFERENCES (PUBLISHED ARTICLES, MANUSCRIPTS, REPORTS, DRAWINGS, PHOTOGRAPHIC RECORDS). CONTACTS: (NAMES & ADDRESSES OF ANYONE WITH EYE-WITNESS ACCOUNTS OR RELEVANT INFORMATION); TAPE RECORDINGS.

SIA NEWSLETTER, vol. 2, no. 2 (March 1973).

12. DANGER OF DEMOLITION OR DAMAGE XX YES □ NO  NATURE OF THREAT:    13. PRIORITY

| 14. EXISTING SURVEYS AND DATES: | □ NHL | X NR 5/9/73 | X HAER stereopairs, 1970 | □ HABS | X STATE Register, 1972 | □ COUNTY | X LOCAL Survey, 1965 | □ OTHER |
|---|---|---|---|---|---|---|---|---|

15. INVENTORIED BY: YOUR NAME   Eric DeLony    ADDRESS    AFFILIATION   HAER    DATE   5/2/73

PLEASE RETURN TO THE HISTORIC AMERICAN ENGINEERING RECORD, NATIONAL PARK SERVICE, WASHINGTON, DC 20240

---

**Cape St. Elias Lighthouse**
Kayak Island
Katalla vicinity
  (UTM: 06.634050.6632175)
The two-story, rectangular lighthouse, of reinforced concrete, was built in 1915. It has had no attendant since 1974.

**Chilkat Oil Refinery Site**
Katalla vicinity
A storage tank, ruined buildings and oil field hardware survive from the first Alaskan refinery, which operated from 1911 to 1933.

**Independence Mines**
Fishook Road
Palmer
Gold was mined at this site intermittently from 1934 to 1950. Sixteen wood-frame buildings survive, all in a deteriorated condition.

## ARIZONA

**Grand Canyon RR Station**
Grand Canyon National Park
Coconino County
The Santa Fe RR built the 1½-story wood station about 1909 and maintained it until 1968; there are apartments, waiting rooms and offices.

**Water Disposal Plant**
Grand Canyon National Park
Coconino County
  (UTM: 12.395930.3989800)
The plant, built in 1926 by the Santa Fe RR, recycled water for toilets, lawns, and the old locomotives' boilers; the site includes filters, tanks and clarifiers.

**Butte-Cochran Charcoal Ovens**
Florence vicinity
  (UTM: 12.484660.3662620)
There are five ovens, built of coursed rubble in about 1890 to produce charcoal in connection with mine reduction works that were active in the region at the time.

**Hohokam Canal**
Horne Street and Consolidated Canal
Mesa (UTM: 12.424200.3700500)
Site includes remains of two irrigation canals built by the Hohokam people, ca. 1200–1400 A.D., and used subsequently by pioneer settlers in the region.

**Roosevelt Dam**
State Route 88
Roosevelt vicinity
This was the world's largest masonry dam when it was built in 1911. It is 284 feet high, and backs up a 17,800-acre reservoir, part of a regional irrigation project.

**Ruby Ghost Town**
Ruby (UTM: 12.477400.3480500)
The site of zinc, lead, copper, silver and gold mining from 1890 to 1940, Ruby is deserted today; there are a dozen dilapidated buildings. Access to the site is restricted.

## ARKANSAS

**Whiteley Water Mill**
State Route 43
Boxley vicinity

The mill is a three-story frame building built in 1870 to house turbine-driven grist-, saw-, and flour mills, and a cotton gin. Some machinery remains.

### Joseph Knoble's Brew House
North 3rd and E Streets
Fort Smith

Built in 1851, the brewery is a three-story stone building containing a beer garden, beer vaults, and brewing equipment; it has been almost fully restored.

### Hoopes Brother & Darlington Wheel Works
Arkansas Village
Jonesboro

Wooden wagon and carriage wheels were produced by this firm from 1867 in Pennsylvania. All the machinery was moved to Jonesboro from the original site.

### U.S. Arsenal
Macarthur Park
Little Rock

A two-story brick building with wooden interior partitions and wooden verandas, the arsenal was built in 1840 as protection from Indians. The interior has been altered very little, and the whole is in excellent condition.

### Crater of Diamonds State Park
Murfreesboro vicinity
(UTM: 15.437850.3765700)

In 1906, diamonds were discovered here, the only known source of the gem in North America. Mining operations have proceeded sporadically since then; the site has yielded about 4,000 diamonds, some of high quality.

### Dollar Way Road
Redfield vicinity

Laid in 1913–14, this was the first rural concrete highway west of the Mississippi, and one of the first highways in the South to use a bituminous seal coat on portland cement; the road was unusual at the time for its uninterrupted length (23.6 miles, originally).

### Wommack Kiln
Wave Road
Wave (UTM: 15.529320.3764160)

This is a pottery kiln, consisting of an arched roof, back and side walls. It was built about 1891. Access to the site is restricted.

## CALIFORNIA

### East Brother Island Light Station
Contra Costa County

The site includes three wooden Victorian buildings, all ca. 1873: light tower/living quarters; boathouse/engine room; and shop/storage room. Though all are in good condition, the station is slated for demolition.

### Folsom Hydroelectric Power System
Folsom vicinity

This was among the first American power systems to provide long-distance, high-voltage, three-phase electric power transmission for significant industrial and municipal use. The site includes a dam and powerhouse.

### Vallejo Flour Mill
Fremont

The wood-frame mill was built in 1841 of stone imported from Spain, and of adobe brick. The frame, some clapboard siding, and the foundations remain.

### Old Fresno Water Tower
2444 Fresno Street
Fresno (UTM: 11.251210.4069350)

The 100-foot tower, finished in 1894, served Fresno until 1963, and stands as a graceful and stately local monument.

### Saline Valley Aerial Tramway
Inyo County (UTM: 11.427225.4061150)

The tramway was built in 1911–12 to carry salt in cable-borne buckets from the Saline Valley to a neighboring valley, over the steepest grades of any tramway-course in the U.S. It ceased operation in 1935. Remains include the tramway's towers.

### Mine Tailing Wheels
Jackson vicinity

There are four wheels, erected in 1912 to carry gold mines' milling residues from the mills to an impounding dam. Each wheel is 68 feet in diameter. The wheels were turned by electric motors. The system was shut down in 1942.

### Remillard Brick Kiln
East Sir Francis Drake Blvd.
Larkspur

The Remillard factories, founded in 1865, produced the bricks that built some of San Francisco's most famous buildings. The kiln, built in 1891, has 16 chambers that form an endless tunnel in an elongated ring. Last used around 1915, the building and kiln are the subject of elaborate restoration and re-use plans.

Vertical Corliss steam engine

### Streetcar Depot
Pershing Avenue and Dewey Avenue
Los Angeles

The wood-frame depot, built ca. 1900, is well maintained, though many original features (e.g., wood shingles and gutters) have been replaced.

### Bale Mill
Highway 29
St. Helena vicinity

The site contains a gristmill, wood-frame with a 40-foot overshot waterwheel and a flume constructed of hollowed-out halves of redwood logs. The mill dates from 1846.

### Union RR Station
1050 Kettner
San Diego

Completed in 1915, the Spanish Renaissance station is noted for its grand scale.

### Albion Brew House
San Francisco

The site includes fresh-water springs, which the brewery utilized from its beginning (ca. 1870) to its close during Prohibition.

### Fire Department Pumping Station
Fort Mason Military Reservation
San Francisco (UTM: 10.550540.4184460)

There are four main pumps, installed in 1910. The pumps are driven by steam turbines. The steam equipment is to be replaced by diesel engines.

### Haslett Warehouse
680 Beach Street
San Francisco (UTM: 10.551150.4184400)

The brick warehouse was built in 1907–9 to store canned vegetables produced by the canneries in the neighborhood: It is embellished with many decorative details, including distinctive iron tie-rod anchor plates.

### Schooner *C. A. Thayer*
State Maritime Historical Park
Hyde Street
San Francisco

The *Thayer* was built in 1895 to carry lumber from sawmills in Washington to California ports. She was one of 122 sailing vessels in that service. From 1912–50, the craft served in the Alaska fisheries.

### Airship Hangars
Valencia and Redhill Avenue
Santa Ana (UTM: 11.423720.3729340)

These two hangars are among the largest wood-supported structures in the world: each is 189 feet high and 1,088 feet long. Each housed six dirigibles. They were built in 1943.

### Knight's Foundry and Shops
13 Eureka Street
Sutter Creek (UTM: 10.692210.4251570)

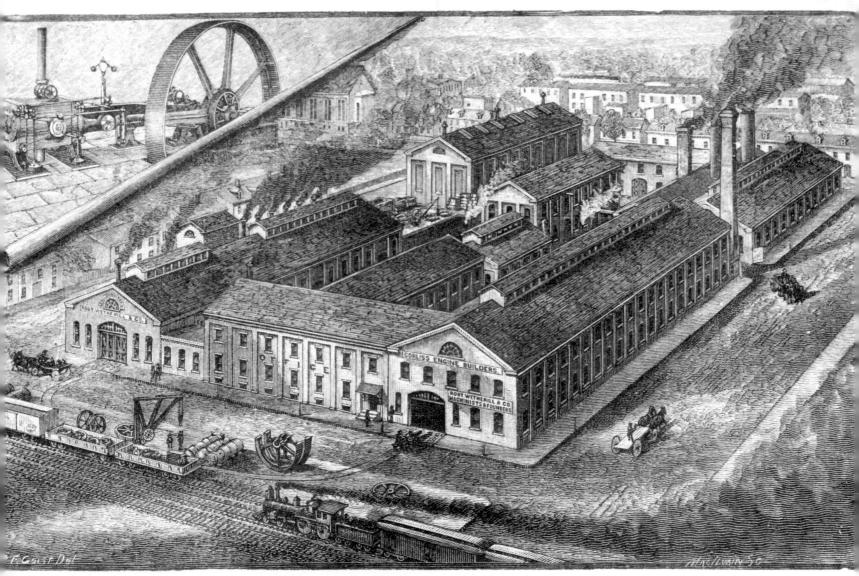

The Robert Wetherell Engine and Machine Works, Chester, Pennsylvania

The site includes a foundry with two cupola iron furnaces, pattern shop, riveting shop, blacksmith shop, and machine shop. The complex was started in 1873 to serve the gold diggings of the Mother Lode. The shops are still powered by water turbines. Access to the site is restricted.

### Key's Desert Queen Ranch
Twentynine Palms vicinity

First buildings date from 1894, but most remains are ca. 1914–16 and include ranch house, sheds, coops, ore loader, water tank, windmill, and miscellaneous machinery. Most buildings are wood shacks in poor condition.

## COLORADO

### Salt Works
Antero Junction vicinity

The site includes a large building with a huge chimney. Salt was produced here from 1865–8, mostly for sale to nearby mills that used it in refining silver ore.

### Register-Call Building
111 Eureka Street
Central City

Built in 1862, when the Register-Call started publication, the stone building still houses some presses from ca. 1865 which are still in use.

### Cokedale Coke Ovens
State Route 12
Cokedale vicinity

The town of Cokedale was built around 1900 to house workers in the busy coal mines and coke works of the region. Beehive ovens survive in a deteriorated condition, along with old machine shops, mine entrances and coal-washing apparatus.

### Corliss Stationary Engine
Western Museum of Mining and Industry
1025 North Gate Road
Colorado Springs

The 36-ton, cross-compound steam engine, built in Providence, Rhode Island, ca. 1895, was used by a paper company in Massachusetts until 1910. It has recently been moved to the Western Museum.

### Narrow-Gauge RR
Durango to Silverton

The route was originally part of the Silverton Branch of the Denver & Rio Grande RR, which built it in 1882 to carry ore, lumber and livestock to mines in the region. This section of the route carries tourists today. RR structures survive at Chama and Alamosa.

### Ruth Rod Mill
Colorado Blvd. at 7th Avenue
Idaho Springs

Joseph P. Ruth built the mill in 1934 for processing gold ore, and ran it until 1952. The mill, now abandoned, used rods to crush ore, rather than a ball system. Ruth's is one of the few surviving rod mills in the U.S.

### Leadville Historic District
Main Street
Leadville

The site includes well-preserved hotels, saloons and other old buildings that have survived the boom-or-bust of the mining town of Leadville for the last 110 years.

### Union Depot
Victoria and B Streets
Pueblo (UTM: 13.533560.4234820)

The rambling red stone depot, in the Romanesque Revival style, was built in 1889–90. A distinctive feature is the large clock tower.

### Royal Gorge Bridge
Arkansas River
Royal Gorge

The Royal Gorge is the highest suspension bridge in the world, running 1,055 feet above the river. Each suspension cable weighs 300 tons. The bridge was built in 1929.

### Moffat Tunnel
U.S. 40
Winter Park vicinity

One of the great engineering feats of this century, the Moffat tunnel was started in 1923 and completed in 1927 at a cost of $18 million and 19 lives. It is 6.2 miles long and carries water as well as the RR tracks for which it was primarily built. The tunnel is still in use.

## CONNECTICUT

### Farmington Canal Lock
487 North Brooksvale Road
Cheshire (UTM: 18.673320.4593320)

The lock, 12 feet wide and 12 feet deep, was built ca. 1828 to accommodate the long (85 feet) canal boats. Gates are missing, but otherwise the site is well preserved. The old gatekeeper's house is now a private residence.

### Collinsville Manufacturing Company
State Route 179
Collinsville vicinity
(UTM: 18.672500.4630500)

Started in 1846, the firm made edged tools. The company's offices are housed in a building, built in 1862, that may be the first portland cement structure in the U.S.

### Cornwall Bridge RR Station
Poppleswamp Brook Road and Kent Road
Cornwall

The old station's board-and-batten siding and slate roof are deteriorating, but inside are many relics of railroad activity: ticket windows, drawers, storage areas and benches. The station was built between 1865 and 1875.

### Merwinsville Station Hotel
Browns Forge Road
Gaylordsville
(UTM: 18.62689.461150)

The hotel was built in 1843 and served rail passengers for many years until faster trains

and Pullman cars made station hotels obsolete.

### Truss Bridge
Riverside Avenue
Greenwich (UTM: 18.618660.4543010)

The double-intersection Whipple truss was built ca. 1865 by the New York, New Haven and Hartford RR to cross the Housatonic River. It was moved to Greenwich in the 1880s. The span is one of America's first iron bridges.

### Holley Manufacturing Company
Pocket Knife Square
Lakeville (UTM: 18.629120.4646690)

The complex of buildings, ca. 1866, is now occupied by the Lakeville Journal. The first pocket knives manufactured in the U.S. came from here.

### Thames Shipyard
Farnsworth Street
New London (UTM: 18.742660.4584660)

The principal features of the site are its system of steam-driven marine railways used for drawing ships from the water, and the two-story brick railway headhouse. An array of steam, electric and rail equipment, mostly ca. 1901, survives.

### Yantic Falls Historic District
Yantic Street
Norwich (UTM: 18.739730.4604800)

The site includes an 1813 nail factory, water-powered textile mills and other factories (ca. 1820s), and a paper mill (1818); the structures are generally in good condition.

### Hitchcock Chair Company
Route 20 at Farmington River
Riverton (UTM: 18.664220.4647340)

Built ca. 1826 as the first Hitchcock chair factory, the building was restored in 1946 for use as a factory and retail store.

### Ponemah Mills
Main Street
Taftville

The mill was one of the largest textile plants in the U.S. It was built in 1866–71 and added to frequently over the next forty years. The site includes the original brick building—an ornate structure with wings, stair towers with belfries, mansard roofs and heavy-timber interior construction.

### Sprain Brook Sawmill
Nettleton Hollow Road
Washington (UTM: 18.644190.4607940)

Dam and mill for this vertical sawmill were originally built in 1756. Rebuilt in 1853 following flood damage, the mill was given a water turbine to replace the old overshot waterwheel. Turbines, vertical shaft and cast-iron gear hardware are still in place.

### Bradway Machine Works
Route 190
West Stafford

The Bradway firm occupied the frame-and-clapboard structure in 1889, but the building dates originally from mid-century or before. The site is particularly notable for its late-nineteenth-century machinery.

## DELAWARE

### Richardson and Roberts Cannery
King's Highway near Budd Street
Dover (UTM: 18.454750.4334450)

The cannery was founded in 1856; the factory building was built in 1881. A belt-driven machine shop is still used, and exhibits of canning and other machinery from the 1880s are on display.

### Agricultural Equipment
Taylor and Messick Company
Harrington (UTM: 18.449090.4307730)

The Taylor and Messick (agricultural equipment) store has on display a collection that includes many tractors and other farm vehicles dating from 1907–20, a hundred gas engines, a diesel engine; and rollers, a corn husker, reapers, thrashers and a conestoga wagon.

### Abbott's Gristmill
Milford vicinity
   (UTM: 18.458670.4304020)

The mill dates from the 1860s, and has hardly been altered. A wealth of milling machinery has also been preserved.

### Curtis Paper Mill
Paper Mill Road
Newark (UTM: 18.435700.4393480)

Standing on the site of an older (ca. 1800) mill, the Curtis operation started in 1848, making fine rag paper. The paper machines, ca. 1880, are still in use.

### Eastburn-Jeanes Limekilns
Paper Mill Road
Newark (UTM: 18.438100.4399280)

There are eight kilns on two sites, built beginning in 1816 and used until after 1900. Most are in excellent condition, and no two are exactly alike. Other features on the site include a gristmill/warehouse, sheds and wheelwright's shop.

### Eleutherian Mills
Hagley Museum
Wilmington (UTM: 18.450900.4403200)

This is the black powder factory founded by E. I. duPont de Nemours in 1801. The site includes a residence, office building (1837), mills and machine shop (1858).

### Hilles & Jones (Machine Tools)
Church and 9th Streets
Wilmington (UTM: 18.453720.4398800)

Two groups of five buildings comprise the site. Some are large and handsome brick structures. Machine tools, engines and boilers, railroad equipment, and drills were produced successively on the site beginning ca. 1858.

### Holly Steam Engine
16th and Market Streets
Wilmington (UTM: 18.453450.4399880)

This vertical three-cylinder steam engine was installed ca. 1902 to pump water for the Wilmington Water Department. It remains in excellent condition.

## DISTRICT OF COLUMBIA

### Bomford's Mill
Potomac and Grace Streets
Georgetown

The brick building was raised in 1845 as a cotton mill, and converted to a flour mill in 1866.

### Castle Gatehouse
Reservoir Road and MacArthur Blvd., N.W.
   (UTM: 18.318780.4308750)

The Gatehouse was erected in 1901 as part of the city's new water-treatment system. The Army Corps of Engineers designed the building to resemble the Corps' insignia.

### East Capitol Street Car Barn
1400 East Capitol Street, N.E.

The site includes a large Romanesque Revival red brick building containing offices and a car house. Built in 1896 to serve the newly-electrified streetcar system, the car barn is empty today.

### Pierce Gristmill
Tilden and Beach Drive, N.W.

The mill was built in 1820 or '29, and thrived during most of the century, shutting down in 1897. It is the last relic of the extensive milling activity that once marked the Rock Creek area.

### Union RR Station
Massachusetts Avenue and 1st Street, N.E.

This is one of the great RR stations in the country (built in 1907–8).

### United Clay Products Company
2801 New York Avenue, N.E.

These brick kilns, which deserve to be one of Washington's premier industrial monuments, operated from 1923 to 1972.

## FLORIDA

### Yulee Sugar Mill
Homosassa vicinity

The mills, now in ruins, operated from 1851 to 1864. During the Civil War, they supplied sugar and syrup to the Confederate Army.

### U.S. Navy Coal Depot
Front and Whitehead Streets
Key West

A brick building with wood-truss construction and buttressed piers, the coal depot was built between 1856 and 1861. Since 1932 it has belonged to the U.S. Coast Guard.

### Herlong Packing Company
Meadow and North 3rd Streets
Leesburg (UTM: 17.41380.318780)

Built in 1929 by a railroad, the concrete-block-and-stucco building is now used for citrus packing by the Herlong firm. Access by permission.

### City Ice Plant
1604 South Harbor City Blvd.
Melbourne (UTM: 17.53880.310580)

A relic of the Florida real estate boom of

the 1920s, the plant was built in 1926. It is of hollow red tile and concrete, with stucco finish. Some of the original equipment is still in use.

### Atlantic Coastline RR Station
1402 Sligh Blvd.
Orlando

Only slightly altered since its construction, the Spanish Mission-style station was built by the Seaboard Coastline RR in 1926.

### Ormond Garage
79 East Granada Avenue
Ormond Beach

The garage opened in 1903 to service autos that used the hard beaches of the region for early speed racing and testing.

### Marine Terminal Building
Barracks and Main Streets
Pensacola

In 1903, when this wood office building was raised by the Louisville & Nashville RR, the company was using Pensacola as a center of trade to the Gulf of Mexico. The building, which has been moved from its original site but is otherwise unchanged, had many novel features when it was built, including electric light and indoor plumbing.

### Miller Shop Water Tower
St. Augustine vicinity

The 150,000-gallon-capacity tank tower was put up in 1925–6 to provide water for the RR yards. It is slated for demolition.

### Bat Tower
River Hills and Cliff Drive
Temple Terrace
   (UTM: 17.36450.310210)

This frame-structure tower was erected ca. 1923 to provide breeding space and shelter for large numbers of bats, which, it was hoped, would keep the local mosquito population in check.

### Standard Cigar Company
2701 North 16th Street
Ybor City

The large brick cigar factory, built in 1900–10, is unusual in having a clock tower.

## GEORGIA

### Street Railway Car Barn
963 Edgewood Street
Atlanta (UTM: 16.74495.373804)

The frame Victorian car barn building was the terminal of the electric Atlanta & Edgewood Street Railroad, founded 1888. The building, adorned with stained glass windows, has been converted to other uses.

**Confederate Chimney**
Goodrich Street at Sibley Mill
Augusta (UTM: 17.40782.370554)

The 168-foot chimney is the only survival from a large gunpowder manufacturing works that flourished here from 1862 to '65. The works were demolished after the Civil War, but the chimney was left standing.

**Canton Cotton Mills**
State Route 5
Canton vicinity
　(UTM: 16.73064.379088)

Still in operation, the mills were founded and built in 1899–1900, and were famous as the source of "Canton Denim."

**Columbus Iron Works**
901 Front Avenue
Columbus (UTM: 16.68825.359346)

Founded ca. 1853, these works supplied cannon for the Confederacy, and served as the principal iron works for the Confederate Navy. Union troops destroyed the works in 1865, but they were soon built up again. The site includes a foundry building, blacksmith shop, and powerhouse.

**Golden Foundry & Machine Company**
600 Twelfth Street
Columbus (UTM: 16.68930.359386)

Begun as a small machine shop in 1882, the Golden firm raised this building in 1890. Additions and alterations were made in 1905, 1969 and 1974.

**Calhoun Mine**
Dahlonega vicinity

The site consists of cuts and tunnels, portals and diggings, made beginning in 1828, when gold mining started in the region.

**McIntosh Sugar Mill**
Kings Bay Army Terminal vicinity
　(UTM: 17.44436.340662)

The mill was opened ca. 1825 to be run by animal power. One floor of the mill house contained a circular walkway for the animals that drove the cane-grinding machinery. The site is a ruin today.

**Rose Hill Mill (Hannah's Mill)**
Hannah's Mill Road at Ten Mile Creek
Upson (UTM: 16.74748.364650)

The rock masonry dam and the three-story wood-frame gristmill were built in 1859. An undershot waterwheel was replaced by a turbine in 1957. The milling equipment was powered by a system of belts and shafts. The site is well preserved.

**McCranie's Turpentine Still**
Willacoochee vicinity

The site includes a cluster of tin-roofed shed-type buildings in which raw gum (resin) was processed into turpentine and rosin between 1936–42. Access to the site is restricted.

# HAWAII
**Ladd & Company Sugar Plantation**
State Route 52
Koloa vicinity (Kauai)

Commercial sugar planting was started here by New Englanders in 1836. A mill building, which used iron rollers, was built on the site in 1841–2. Stone foundations are the only remains.

# IDAHO
**Union Pacific Mainline Depot**
1701 Eastover Terrace
Boise

The depot, in the Spanish colonial style with white stucco walls and orange roof tiles, was built in 1925. It has three main elements: waiting room block, office wing, and campanile with chimes.

**Camas Prairie RR Trestle**
U.S. Route 95
Craigmont

A heavy-timber trestle with wooden cross-bracing and cribs. The trestle construction includes 20–25 bents.

**Charcoal Kilns**
Idaho Falls vicinity

Four kilns remain of 16 that produced charcoal for mine smelters in the region between 1885–9. Kilns are 20 feet high and 21½ feet across.

**Silver City Historic District**
Owyhee County

Gold and silver discoveries in 1862–4 produced a mining boom town at Silver City that began to decline in the '80s. Buildings date from ca. 1884. There are mining remains, including dumps, mill sites, shafts and tunnels.

# ILLINOIS
**Chicago Avenue Water Tower**
North Michigan Avenue
Chicago (UTM: 16.448250.4638330)

The stone tower, in castellated Gothic style, was raised in 1869 along with a similar pumping station, to pump water from Lake Michigan for the Chicago water system, then one of the country's most advanced. The tower is one of the few buildings to survive the Chicago Fire of 1871.

**Pullman Historic District**
Cottage Grove Avenue and 103rd Street
Chicago

In the first major effort in America to create a completely planned model industrial town, George Pullman had the complex built between 1880–4 to house workers in the Pullman RR car factories. The site is preserved in good condition.

**Illinois and Michigan Canal**
Chicago to Lasalle

The 100-mile canal was begun in 1836 and completed in 1848. It was a factor in the prosperity of Chicago. Commercial use ended in 1933. Some of the canal's locks are still in working order.

**Ryan Round Barn**
Route 78
Kewanee vicinity

Built in 1910, the distinctive frame barn is 61 feet high and 74 feet in diameter. It has a central silo 11 feet in diameter. The whole sits on a reinforced concrete foundation.

**Graue Gristmill**
York and Spring Roads
Oak Brook (UTM: 16.422840.4630090)

The three-story brick mill was built between 1847–52, and operated until 1952. It has been converted into a museum. Milling and driving machinery are intact.

**Rock Island Arsenal**
Rock Island

Ten massive stone shops and ten other buildings form the old nucleus of the modern arsenal. The arsenal was built in 1864 and originally manufactured cups, saddle studs and brass rings for the Army.

# INDIANA
**Cannelton Cotton Mills**
Front and 4th Streets
Cannelton (UTM: 16.522380.4195810)

Built between 1849–50, the three-story towered mill produced plain cotton sheeting for 100 years. The building's walls are of rubble masonry, faced with hewn sandstone. Considered lavish when it was new, the mill is also ingeniously utilitarian.

**City Market**
222 East Market Street
Indianapolis

The market consists of a central unit (1886), red brick with limestone trim, and two wings (1903). The 200-foot-long central portion is laid out as a nave with side aisles.

**Duesenberg Factory**
West Washington and Harding Streets
Indianapolis

In the 1920s and '30s, the famous racing autos were made on the site, which today contains two office buildings and two factories, steel-frame with brick exterior walls.

**Spring Mill (Village State Park)**
State Route 60
Mitchell vicinity

First settled in 1816–17, the village centered around a stone mill run by an overshot waterwheel. The village prospered until 1850, when it was bypassed by the railroads.

**American Car & Foundry Company**
Missouri Street
New Albany

The site includes several long brick sheds with corbelled cornices, and a four-story building with a stair tower. The plant was built ca. 1872 and continued to produce RR cars until 1950.

# IOWA
**Delta Covered Bridge**
North Skunk River

Coal tipple at the Cascade, West Virginia, coke works

Delta vicinity (UTM: 15.556680.4571960)
The 80-foot span has timber Burr truss construction and rests on three piers, one of limestone slabs and the others of steel caissons filled with concrete. The bridge was built in 1869.

### Bernatz Mill
200 North Mill Street
Decorah

The stone mill was raised between 1851–3 and made flour by water power until 1947. Roller milling equipment replaced stone grinding wheels on the site in 1875. The mill has been extensively altered.

### Wapsipinicon Mill
100 First Street West
Independence

Built in 1867 as a woolen mill, the building was used as a feed mill, and later was adapted to produce electricity for the community.

### Round Barn
Rural Route 1
West Liberty

The Secrest-Ryan octagon barn is a board-and-batten structure resting on a limestone foundation. It has three levels: lower for livestock, ground-floor for machinery, upper for hay. The levels are connected by a hanging "railway" conveyor system.

## KANSAS

### RR Repair Shops
Horton vicinity

The site was one of the principal sites for the repair of steam locomotives and RR cars of the Chicago, Rock Island & Pacific RR. Some of the buildings are used today by a contracting company.

**Blacksmith and Wheelwright Shop**
Fort Larned
Larned

Built in 1868 of sandstone rubble, the building still contains its old forge.

**Union Pacific Depot**
Third Street
Solomon

The depot was built in 1885. It is of limestone, trimmed with wood in the Victorian manner.

**Schonhoff Windmill**
City Park
Wamego

The red sandstone windmill was built by a Dutch immigrant on his farm in 1879. It was used to grind feed and flour for about ten years. The mill was subsequently moved to its present site.

# KENTUCKY

**Covington–Cincinnati Bridge**
U.S. Routes 25 and 42
Covington (UTM: 16.715360.4329840)

John A. Roebling designed this iron-frame truss suspension bridge over the Ohio River in 1856. The bridge's total span is 1,057 feet. It has been added to and altered somewhat over the years.

**Fitchburg Iron Furnace**
Daniel Boone National Forest
Fitchburg

The furnace was unique in that it consisted of two furnaces in one structure. Built in 1868 of stone, it was 65 feet high and 115 feet long—reputedly the largest furnace of its kind in the world when it was built.

**Penn Central RR Bridge**
Ohio River between Jeffersonville and
    Louisville

The present bridge (1910) replaced an earlier span (1870) that marked an important step forward in the development of the long-span truss. The original piers remain.

**Steamer** *Belle of Louisville*
City Wharf
Louisville

The *Belle* is a Mississippi River stern-wheel steamboat, built in 1914 and one of the last in operation.

**Bourbon Stockyards**
1048 East Main Street
Louisville

The site comprises several long sheds, built in 1907 when meat-packing was an important enterprise in Louisville. There are slaughter- and packing houses, and yards. The complex has a spectacular brick gateway trimmed with Baroque terra-cotta ornaments.

**Crescent Hill Reservoir and Pumping Station**
Reservoir Avenue
Louisville

The pumphouse and superintendent's house

(1876–9) are examples of the high Victorian Gothic design. The site includes four Allis-Chalmers vertical, triple-expansion steam engines which have been operational since the 1900s.

**RR Freight Terminal**
103 North Preston Street
Louisville

The two-story brick Romanesque Revival office building was built ca. 1900 by the Chesapeake & Ohio RR. It fronts a large steel-frame train shed.

**Wolf Pen Branch Mill**
Wolf Pen Branch Road
Louisville

The mill, a typical gristing operation, was in continuous use from 1820–30 until recently. Its machinery remains intact, though the 26-foot wooden waterwheel has been disconnected.

# LOUISIANA

**Enterprise Plantation**
Patoutville
Jeanerette (UTM: 15.623020.3308540)

The first sugar mill on the site was built in 1829, a plantation house followed in 1835. The site also includes a canal system, dredged in the 1870s, that gave the plantation access to the Gulf of Mexico.

**Leeds Iron Foundry**
923 Tchoupitoulas Street
New Orleans (UTM: 15.783020.3315860)

Established in 1825, the foundry was the first in the city. The Gothic Revival building was built in 1852, has an exterior of stuccoed brick, and cast-iron columns. Leeds Foundry made cotton bale presses, and cannon and iron-clad shipping for the Confederacy.

**St. Charles Streetcar Line**
New Orleans (UTM: 15.782590.3315900)

The St. Charles line is the oldest continuously operated street railway in the world, having begun service in 1895. It covers 13.4 miles of track in the city, and presently uses steel "arch-roof" type car built by the Brill & Perly Thomas Car Co., High Point, North Carolina.

**Screw Pumps**
"Melpomene" Pumping Station
New Orleans

Installed in numbers around 1915, the low-head, high-volume axial screw pumps like those on this site were used to clear the city's low places of storm water.

# MAINE

**Kennebec Arsenal**
Arsenal Street
Augusta

Built in 1828, the arsenal produced ammunition and other military wares until it was closed in 1903; thereafter the building was used as an insane asylum by the State of Maine.

**Percy & Small Shipyard**
Washington Street

Bath (UTM: 19.434400.4860230)

Opened in 1896, this yard produced the last commercially significant wooden sailing ships in the U.S. It reached peak production between 1900–9, when it built 22 schooners, including some six-masters. The last launching from P & S was in 1920. The Bath Marine Museum maintains the yard today.

**Sunday River Bridge**
Bethel vicinity

This 100-foot-long covered bridge consists of a single span supported by two flanking timber Paddleford trusses and resting on granite block abutments on either bank of the river. It was constructed ca. 1872 and used until 1955.

**Katadhin Iron Works**
Brownville Junction vicinity

Iron ore was discovered in the region in 1843. The iron works opened in 1845 and continued operations until 1890. The site was restored in 1966.

**Perkins Tide Mill**
Mill Lane off North Street
Kennebunkport

Perkins' gristmill, powered by the motion of the tides, was built in 1749 and ran until 1939. It is wood-frame with coursed-rubble and wood-pile foundations. Most of the milling equipment is intact; the building has been converted into a restaurant.

**Suspension Bridge**
New Portland

The 188-foot wire bridge over the Carrabassett River here is the second oldest surviving suspension bridge in the U.S. Tower framing, main cables and anchorages are original; other components are later. The bridge was built ca. 1850–60

**Portland Stove Foundry.**
57 Kennebec Street
Portland (UTM: 19.398325.4834900)

Manufacturing techniques have changed little in the Portland Foundry's complex of Victorian brick and wood-frame buildings, erected in 1880. Molten iron is still ladeled by hand into stove molds each day, in a process described as early as 1899.

**Portland Breakwater Light**
Harbor
South Portland

Built in 1855 and rebuilt twenty years later, the light tower is of brick filler covered with cast-iron plates. There is Greek Revival ornamentation.

**Cumberland Mills Historic District**
Westbrook

A good example of a nineteenth-century planned industrial community, the site contains Queen Anne mill worker's housing, a community hall, and a hotel. The S. D. Warren Company produced wood pulp on the site; the concern was especially prosperous around 1870.

Main Street Railroad Station, Richmond

## MARYLAND

### Thomas Point Shoals Light Station
Kent Island, Chesapeake Bay
Annapolis

The wood-frame station is hexagonal, 18 feet on a side, and stands on steel screw pilings.

### Baltimore & Ohio Passenger Car Shop
Pratt and Poppleton Streets
Baltimore (UTM: 18.359160.4349510)

This 22-sided building, probably the largest "round" industrial structure in the world, is 235 feet across, and 123 feet high. It was built in 1883–4 as a repair shop for the B & O's passenger cars, and served that purpose until 1963, when it was converted into a railroad museum.

### Baltimore & Ohio Viaduct
Gwynn's Falls near Carroll Park
Baltimore (UTM: 18.357220.4348440)

The first masonry RR bridge in the U.S., the bridge is 297 feet long, and rests on a full centered arch that spans the river, with masonry walled approaches on each bank. It was built in 1828–9, and has been in service ever since.

### Catoctin Furnace Historic District
U. S. Route 15
Catoctin Furnace

The site of iron works from 1774 to 1904.

Two furnaces (one built in 1853), workers cottages, race ditches, iron control gates, and various dams are features of the site.

### Chesapeake and Delaware Canal Pumphouse
Chesapeake City
(UTM: 18.430625.4375400)

The first pumping station on the site was built in 1837 to supply water for the canal. New equipment was installed in 1851, including a lift wheel 38 feet across, and the first of two 175-horsepower beam engines that remained in service until 1927.

### Baltimore & Ohio RR Station
at Patapsco Road Bridge
Ellicott City

This oblong, two-story stone building, built in 1830–1, is the oldest RR station in the country. Its exterior is practically unchanged.

### Baltimore & Ohio RR Station
Point of Rocks (UTM: 18.281450.4349960)

This station was built in the mid-1870s by the B & O to serve the junction of its metropolitan Potomac Valley line with its middle-western line. The facade, brick with horizontal bands of granite stripping, and the lancet windows with decorative stonework, make this building one of the outstanding works of the Victorian Gothic Revival in America.

### Baltimore & Ohio RR Thomas Viaduct
Patapsco River Valley
Relay (UTM: 18.352060.4342500)

In use since its construction in 1835, this 612-foot span is the oldest RR viaduct in the U.S. It is composed of eight semicircular arches, in stone.

## MASSACHUSETTS

### Old Schwamb Mill
17 Mill Lane
Arlington

The Schwamb family made picture frames on the site starting in 1847. The site includes the main factory (ca. 1860) with the old lathes, tools, and belt-and-pulley system; the wood-drying kiln; and a wood storage barn whose basement held the waterwheel that drove the factories. Ells were added to the main building ca. 1870 and ca. 1900.

### Lincoln Power Station Coal Bunker
464 Commercial Street
Boston

The heavy-timber bunker received coal from ships and stored it for use by the nearby power plant.

### Charlton Mill
Howe and Crawford Streets
Fall River

131

Built in 1910, this was the last granite textile mill erected in Fall River. Its unusual width (374 feet) and large window area represent a refinement of mill building design.

### Davol Mills
Rodman Street and Plymouth Avenue
Fall River

The two old cotton-textile mills, built in 1867 and 1871, are brick with mansard roofs, and have four stories above the ground floor. Accessory structures—a boiler house and storehouse dating from 1890–1909—are also on the site.

### Durfee Mills
Plymouth Avenue and Pleasant Street
Fall River

The site comprises buildings, including three mills built between 1866–80. The mills are of granite, with gable roofs that were wood shingled originally. Office buildings, boiler houses and engine rooms are also on the site, once the most impressive mill complex in Fall River.

### Hoosac Tunnel
Florida–North Adams

About twelve trains per day still pass through the tunnel, which was among the first projects of its kind undertaken in the U.S. Begun in 1858, the five-mile tunnel was finished in 1875 (work halted during 1861–2). The tunnel was built for the Troy & Greenfield RR.

### Washington House and Machine Shop
Hancock

Built in 1790 by members of a Shaker community, the frame-and-clapboard building remained in use as a laundry, machine shop and sawmill, until this century.

### Holyoke Power Canal System
Holyoke (UTM: 18.697550.4675000)

The original canal was designed in 1794. It was ten miles long, and was equipped with locks and inclined planes. There is little remaining evidence of the planes, which hauled boats in wooden caissons operated by two 16-foot waterwheels.

### Lawrence Machine Shop (Everett Mills)
Union Street near Canal Street
Lawrence

Built in 1846–8 as a shop to repair machinery in the Lawrence textile mills, the building was itself converted to a mill in 1861. The heavy timber construction, with load-bearing exterior walls and cast-iron interior columns, water gates and associated machinery, and two turbines and generators (ca. 1930) are preserved.

### Pemberton Mill
Union Street near Canal Street
Lawrence

The six-story mill building has continuous clerestory windows and decorative gambrel roofs on the central towers of the east and west elevations. Built in 1861, the structure is a good example of mid-nineteenth-century mill construction.

### Boott Mills
Amory Street
Lowell (UTM: 19.310800.472410)

The mills were established in 1835, and by 1848 were producing 10.5 million yards of cloth per year. The six original buildings (1835–43) still stand, though the original clerestory monitor roofs have been replaced by an additional story. The mills were powered by waterwheels and turbines driven by Lowell's Eastern Canal, though steam engines were also used.

### Eastern Canal
Parallels Bridge and French Streets
Lowell (UTM: 19.310750.472368)

The canal was constructed in 1835 to power the Prescott, Massachusetts, and Boott Mills. It runs for 2,037 feet, and averages 8 feet in depth and 40–65 feet in width. The Eastern is one element in Lowell's complex of power canals, which comprises a total of about five miles of waterways in some seven canals. The system remains intact, though canal machinery (locks, dams, etc.) is often deteriorated.

### Lawrence Manufacturing Company
Perkins Street
Lowell (UTM: 19.310160.472460)

Dating from 1831, the firm was producing up to 13.5 million yards of cloth annually by 1848. The mills included 105,000 spindles in the latter year. Power came from Lowell's Lawrence Canal, and from steam engines. Two of the original (1832) mill buildings remain, though—as at the Boott Mills—they have been altered by the addition of a story.

### United States Cartridge Company
687 Lawrence Street
Lowell (UTM: 19.311170.472228)

Established in 1869, the firm produced small arms ammunition in the three-story wood-frame building, 150 feet by 30. All power came from steam engines. One of the first manufacturers of wholly self-contained rifle ammunition, the company prospered during the First World War, and ceased operations afterward. The original building, built in 1865, survives.

### Granite Railway Incline
Mullin Avenue
Quincy

About a third of the incline (130 feet), which was constructed in 1830 to give access to a granite quarry, remains. The railway system of which the incline was a part was the first railway to be commercially used in the U.S. It started with horse-drawn cars in 1826; later, movement of the cars was controlled by a chain or pulley.

### Saugus Iron Works National Historic Site
Saugus

The first successful iron works in the Colonies, the Saugus operation opened in 1644 and produced pig-, wrought-, and rod-iron, as well as iron ware, until 1665. Restored beginning in 1917, the site includes an ironmaster's house, a museum of iron artifacts, and a blast furnace.

### Springfield Armory
Federal Square
Springfield

Established in 1794, this is the country's oldest working arsenal, and is today a main Army center for the development of small arms. The first permanent building was the West Arsenal (1807). Middle Arsenal followed in 1830.

### Boston & Maine RR Station
North Hoosac Road and Southworth Street
Williamstown

The depot, of rough hewn Vermont bluestone, with a low hipped roof, is the only remnant of a once-flourishing RR site in Williamstown. It was built in 1898.

## MICHIGAN

### Grand Trunk RR Station
25 East Dickman Street
Battle Creek (UTM: 16.650460.4685820)

The Grand Trunk depot, built in 1905, is a three-story building with stone walls on the first level, brick walls above. It is adorned with two square bell towers, and its main lobby, 100 feet by 60 feet, is distinguished by massive wooden roof-support arches.

### Belding Brothers Mill No. 1
Ashfield and Riverside Streets
Belding

The three-story, red brick mill was built in 1889 and used exclusively for the manufacture of silk thread. Raw silk was spun into thread on the first floor; the thread was wound on the second floor, and spooled on the third. Three hundred were employed in the mill at its peak of activity. The mill closed in 1934.

### Calumet and Hecla Industrial District
Calumet

The Calumet & Hecla mining company, incorporated in 1871, was noted for high quality copper and enlightened labor practices: workers were treated with unusual consideration, as the presence of a workers' library and bathhouse on the site attests. Other structures on the site, all of which date from 1880–1910, include a machine shop, blacksmith shop, roundhouse, warehouse, boilerhouse and gearhouse.

### Pewabic Pottery Company
10125 East Jefferson Avenue
Detroit (UTM: 17.336815.4691610)

The building is a two-story structure, timber and brick below, half-timbered stucco above. It houses a system of belts, drive wheels and beveled pinnion gears, which drove the pottery making machinery. Built in 1907, the building is still used, for pottery classes and as a museum.

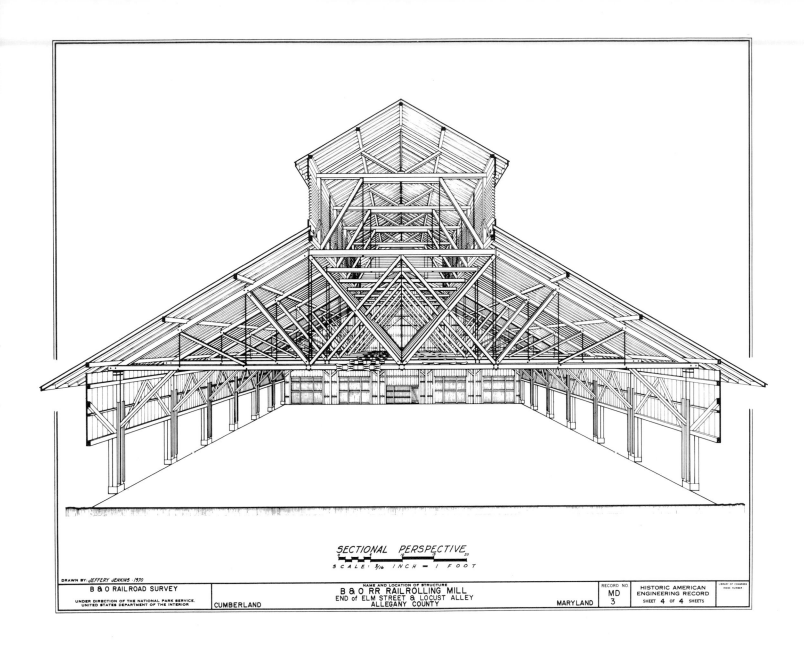

SECTIONAL PERSPECTIVE

SCALE: 3/16 INCH = 1 FOOT

DRAWN BY: JEFFERY JENKINS · 1970

B & O RAILROAD SURVEY

UNDER DIRECTION OF THE NATIONAL PARK SERVICE.
UNITED STATES DEPARTMENT OF THE INTERIOR

CUMBERLAND

NAME AND LOCATION OF STRUCTURE
B & O RR RAILROLLING MILL
END of ELM STREET & LOCUST ALLEY
ALLEGANY COUNTY

MARYLAND

RECORD NO
MD
3

HISTORIC AMERICAN
ENGINEERING RECORD
SHEET 4 OF 4 SHEETS

LIBRARY OF CONGRESS
INDEX NUMBER

**Detroit Cornice and Slate Company Building**
733 St. Antoine at East Lafayette Street
Detroit (UTM: 17.331880.4688720)
Built in 1897, the three-story brick building is notable for its front facade of hammered and pressed galvanized steel—complete with friezes and tympanums—all painted to resemble stone. The Detroit Cornice firm vacated the building in 1972, and the new owners hope to convert it in a scheme of adaptive re-use.

**Flowerfield Mills**
Factory Street
Flowerfield (UTM: 16.611000.4657780)
Built in 1855, the three-story gristmill contains equipment for three distinct milling processes. There is a 48-inch-diameter stone for producing stone-ground flour, six rolling machines for finer flour, and a "hammer mill" for feed grains. The mill, powered by water until 1913, ceased operation in 1943.

**Alabaster Mine**
1200 Judd Street, S.W.

Grand Rapids (UTM: 16.605130.4754960)
The mine was opened in 1907, to exploit gypsum deposits that had been discovered as early as 1827. It extends to six miles of tunnels, 85 feet below the surface. The mine closed in 1943, and the tunnels are now used by a storage company.

**Grand Rapids Water Filtration Plant**
1430 Monroe Street, N.E.
Grand Rapids (UTM: 16.608440.4760250)
The plant is a two-story brick building with tile roofs, and is in an essentially unchanged condition. The system was completed in 1912 and expanded in 1924.

**Nordberg (Milwaukee) Hoisting Engine**
Quincy Copper Mine
Hancock
Installed to turn a cable drum that brought ore 9,260 feet up from the deep mine, this is the largest steam hoist ever built. It was powered by four Corliss steam cylinders in an inverted V arrangement. The hoist was derelict from 1931–66. It has since been

recognized as a monument and preserved.

**"Federal Aid Bridge"**
U.S .Route 12, St. Joseph River
Mottville (UTM: 16.603045.4628005)
The bridge is a three-span, concrete girder structure, 270 feet long, built in 1922.

**Old Presque Isle Lighthouse**
Presque Isle Harbor (Lake Huron)
The lighthouse is a 30-foot round tower, made of brick and stone, with a circular dressed-stone staircase inside. Built by the U.S. Government in 1840 as a coast and harbor light, it has been renovated and fitted with a new lamp and lamphouse (1961).

**St. Mary's Falls Canal: Soo Locks**
Sault Ste. Marie
The canal was built in 1852–5 to bypass rapids obstructing transport to and from copper mines in the Upper Peninsula of Michigan. There were originally two 350-foot locks, since gone. Two more locks were added between 1914–19.

Smithfield Street Bridge, Pittsburgh

## MINNESOTA

### Aerial Lift Bridge
Duluth Ship Canal, Lake Avenue
Duluth (UTM: 15.569260.5180790)

Designed in 1899 as a transporting bridge, the 394-foot span could carry a load of 125,000 pounds on a moving platform powered by electric batteries. In 1929, the bridge was modified to accommodate automobile traffic. The old platform was replaced with a counter-weighted electric-powered lift-bridge.

### Duluth Union Depot
Fifth Avenue West and Michigan Street
Duluth

The French Chateau style station is an excellent example of the majestic tradition in RR stations that grew up at the time it was built (late 1880s).

### Phelps Mill
County Road 45
Maine vicinity

The water-powered mill complex (ca. 1889) consists of a flour mill, buckwheat/rye mill, turbine houses, and dam. The flour mill is framed with hand-hewn timbers and covered with wood clapboards. Much of the original machinery remains in place, though the mill last operated in 1939.

### Burlington Northern RR Bridge
Mississippi River
Minneapolis

"One of the finest stone viaducts in the world." The stone-arch span is 2,100 feet long and 76 feet high; it is supported by 23 circular stone arches of varying lengths. The bridge was built in 1883.

### Pillsbury A Mill
Main and 3rd Streets, S.E.
Minneapolis

When it was built in 1880, this was the largest flour mill in the world. It is 180 feet long and 117 feet high. The mill, which is still in use, is closed to the public.

### Como Park Conservatory
Como Park
Saint Paul (UTM: 15.488100.4980740)

The greenhouses, capable of holding 100,000 plants, are constructed in a glass-and-iron-frame style typical among buildings of the type at the time this one was built (1914–15).

### Soudan Mine
near State Routes 1 and 169
Tower-Soudan vicinity

An engine house, drill house, crusher shop and dry house survive on the site of what was the deepest (2,500 feet) iron mine in Minnesota's rich Vermillion range. At peak production ca. 1892, the mine employed 1,800.

## MISSISSIPPI

### U.S.S. *Cairo*
Ingalls Ship Yard
Pascagoula

The *Cairo* is an ironclad warship built for the U.S. Navy in 1861. It served in the Civil War until it was sunk in 1862. The hulk was raised in 1965 and awaits restoration.

### Buena Vista Cotton Gin
Port Gibson vicinity

Constructed in ca. 1848 to be driven by horses, the gin was converted to steam power in the period 1857–61. All that remains at the site is a 50-foot brick smokestack.

### Textile Building
Mississippi State University
Starkville

Mississippi's legislature established the textile training school at Mississippi State in 1900, and raised this building to house a "miniature cotton factory for instruction in all the details" of cotton textile manufacture. The school closed in 1914.

## MISSOURI

### Bonne Terre Mine
Highway 47
Bonne Terre

Beginning in 1865, lead was mined on a large scale at Bonne Terre, 35 million tons having been removed when the digging stopped in 1962. Five shafts were sunk, and a 13-mile narrow-gauge RR was put in. There are no above-ground remains today.

### Old Stone Hill Historic District
401 Twelfth Street
Hermann

Old stone hill is the site of a winery, and includes a residence/office, processing plant, warehouse, barn, and aging cellars. Established in 1869, the winery still operates.

### Burfordville Mill
Highway 34
Jackson vicinity

Built in 1867–8 on the site of an older mill, this gristmill is of squared rubble masonry in the first floor, and of brick in the three stories above. It was powered by water turbines. Inside, much original machinery remains. The mill closed in 1942, but is now being restored.

### Watkins Mill Complex
Lawson vicinity

"The best preserved example of a mid-nineteenth-century woolen mill in the U.S." Built in 1860, the three-story brick mill, powered by steam, operated until the end of the century. Original textile machines, some of which survive nowhere else, are in place at Watkins Mill.

### Maramee Iron Works District
St. James vicinity

Missouri iron was important in American industry until the 1870s, when the huge iron deposits around Lake Superior became known. The Maramee complex opened in 1829 and operated until 1877. The buildings survive in good condition.

### Anheuser-Busch Brewery
721 Pestalozzi Street
St. Louis

Anheuser-Busch is the firm that perfected pasteurization of beer, which permitted beer to be distributed widely. On this site the oldest structures are an administration building (1868), stables (1885), and brew house (1891–2). All have elaborate brick construction, with ornamental gargoyles and other fancies.

### Bissell Street Water Tower
Bissell Street and Blair Avenue
St. Louis

The 195-foot tower is of brick, stone and terra-cotta, and was built in 1885–6 to house a standpipe to serve St. Louis' water mains. Out of use since 1913, the tower is to be condemned.

### Eads Bridge
Washington Avenue
St. Louis

James B. Eads designed and built the three-arch bridge over the Mississippi (1868–74), employing several new materials and building techniques. This is one of the earliest bridges to use hollow (tubular) construction members that were all steel. Tubes are joined by a dense system of diagonal braces. Of the two decks on the span, the upper carries auto traffic; the lower, now closed, was used by trains.

### Water Intake Towers
Mississippi River, Chain of Rocks Bridge
St. Louis

The two stone buildings stand in the river channel, guarded by massive stone prows that protect them from ice and floating logs. They house the gates that admit water to tunnels in the river bed. The water passes ultimately into the St. Louis water system. Tower No. 1 (1894) is in the Romanesque Revival style; No. 2 is Renaissance Revival. Both are used today as standby equipment.

### McMormick Distillery
Highway JJ
Weston

The site includes a spring, distillery building made of limestone rubble (1857), and caves in which whiskey is aged. The business remains active, having operated since 1858 (with a hiatus, ca. 1919–33).

## NEBRASKA

### Woral Smith Limestone Kiln and House
Fairbury vicinity
  (UTM: 14.650550.4450880)

Limestone was kiln-fired to burn off impurities and to make it soft for use as mortar and whitewash. Smith's kiln was built in 1874. Two years later, he built his house, 1½ stories high, entirely of limestone.

### Rock Island Depot
1944 O Street
Lincoln

Built in 1892–3, the depot, in the Chateau style, is of red sandstone and brick.

### Burlington RR Headquarters
1004 Farnam Street
Omaha (UTM: 15.254580.4571290)

Now a warehouse for the Weiner International Tire & Rubber Co., the old Burlington and Missouri River headquarters, in the Italiante style, was completed in 1879 and remodeled in 1886 and '89. A pyramidal skylight covers a courtyard that penetrates the second, third and fourth floors.

### Cook Blacksmith Shop
204 Third Street
Ponca (UTM: 14.688190.4714580)

Built in 1901, and in operation for thirty years, Cook's shop is a fine example of a western blacksmith shop. The one-story frame building, as well as much equipment, are preserved in good condition.

## NEVADA

### RR Shops
North Stewart and Ann Streets
Carson City

The rectangular, one-story shops, 183 by 312 feet, were maintained by the Virginia & Truckee RR. Today they are dilapidated.

### Ward Charcoal Ovens
Cave Valley Road
Ely vicinity

The site includes six stone ovens built in 1876. Each is 30 feet high, with an arched roof made of stones fitted together so that the roof holds up with no supporting members. The kilns produced charcoal for mine smelters.

### Eureka Historic District
Eureka

Ten smelter sites, stone, frame and brick houses, hotels, blacksmith shops, churches and an opera house are among the remains of this silver boom town, which flourished in 1871–85. The last mine was closed in 1970.

### U.S. Bureau of Reclamation Newlands Project
U.S. Route 80, Truckee River
Sparks vicinity

Begun in 1903 and completed in 1913, the project included four dams, 104 miles of canals, reservoirs and power plants. The primary purpose of the project was to provide irrigation water for the arid region.

## NEW HAMPSHIRE

### Gas Works
South Main Street
Concord (UTM: 19.294320.4785440)

The gas works at Concord are the best preserved in the U.S. The complex (ca. 1888) includes a brick gasholder house, iron gasholder, 10-sided oil house, tar pit, pumphouse and purification plant.

### Cornish-Windsor Covered Bridge
Connecticut River at Cornish
  (UTM: 18.711570.4816540)

This is the longest (460 feet) covered bridge in the U.S. It is a two-span, Towne Lattice timber truss, built in 1866 and still in service.

### Steel Arch Bridge
Connecticut River at Walpole

The parabolic arch bridge, 540 feet long, spans the Connecticut River. It was built in 1905. The bridge is closed today.

### Contoocook Mills Industrial District
Mill Street
Hillsboro (UTM: 19.264550.4777250)

Saw, grist and cotton mills used the Contoocook River's power on this site in the 1700s and early 1800s. The site presently contains six brick mill buildings ca. 1845, 1865, some of which still produce textiles.

### Belknap-Sulloway Mill
Mill Street
Laconia

Built in 1823, and at that time the nucleus of a small manufacturing village, this brick textile mill is one of the oldest in its area.

### Busiel-Seeburg Mill
Mill Street
Laconia

Stockings were made here from ca. 1853.

The mill is now the center of an urban renewal project in the area.

### Amoskeag Millyard
Canal Street
Manchester

At one time the site was the largest textile mill complex in the world, stretching for more than a mile along the Merrimack River. The buildings in the complex were built between 1838–1915, and include the remnants of a paper mill, bleach and dye house, and six textile mills.

## NEW JERSEY

### Franklin Corners Historic District
Hardscrabble Road
Bernards Township

A small farm and mill village dating mostly from the early and mid-1800s. Notable buildings include Van Dorn's flour mill (1842–3) and McMurtry's sawmill (ca. 1828).

### Delaware and Raritan Canal
Bordentown to New Brunswick

The canal was built between 1830–4 to give the Pennsylvania coal fields access to the Port of New York. It was 43 miles long, incorporated 14 locks, and carried 2.3 million tons of coal in 1866, its best year. The canal was last operated in 1932.

### Village of Allaire
State Route 324
Farmingdale vicinity

The site includes remains of a deserted village that grew up ca. 1822 around a foundry where bog iron from the region was worked. Remains of an iron furnace, casting house, gristmill, sawmill, carpenter's shop and church are on the site, as well as other evidence.

### Truss Bridge
County Route 2
Hamden (UTM: 18.508240.4494580)

The Trenton Locomotive & Machine Manufacturing Co. built this cast-iron Fink truss bridge in 1857. It is about 100 feet long and 19 feet high. The span combines several systems of triangular bracing.

### Lakehurst Naval Air Station
Lakehurst

Between 1921, when it was opened, and ca. 1937, the station was a base for dirigibles or zeppelin-type airships, which were housed in its seven huge hangars. The largest hangar is 12 stories high and 807 feet long. The station today is unused.

### Eastern Charcoal Company
State Route 40
Mays Landing

Production of charcoal for fuel was an important industry in Southern New Jersey in the late 1800s. At this site, which closed in 1965, remains include 50-foot towers, huge yellow brick beehive ovens, and a quantity of tools and equipment.

### Speedwell Village
333 Speedwell Avenue
Morristown

The site of iron-industry activity in the 1700s, factories at Speedwell produced paddle wheels and other machinery for early steamboats (1818). It was also here (1838) that the telegraph was perfected by Samuel F. B. Morse and Alfred Vail (at Vail's factory on the site).

### Paterson Great Falls
Paterson

The first planned industrial complex in the U.S., Paterson grew up around the water power provided by the falls. Since 1793, local industries have included (among those of which remains survive): an 1803 paper making mill; an 1812 cotton mill; and Colt's gun factory (1835–6).

### Water Turbine
Morris Canal
Stewartsville vicinity

The only turbine of the Scotch or Baker (Reaction) type known to remain in situ in the U.S. The turbine is ca. 1850. It powered the winding gear that hauled boats up an inclined plane on the Morris Canal.

### Edison National Historical Site
Main Street and Lakeside Avenue
West Orange

Thomas Edison moved his research laboratories to this site in 1887. Edison's motion picture house (in reproduction), and many

Interior detail, Shoshone Power Plant, Buffalo Bill Dam, Cody, Wyoming

Cannelton, Indiana, Cotton Mill

notebooks and other records, are preserved here.

## NEW MEXICO

### Ilfield Company Warehouse
200 First Street, N.W.
Albuquerque (UTM: 13.349900.3883530)

The Charles Ilfield Company built this warehouse, an early steel and reinforced concrete building in a square courtyard layout, in 1911. It is one of the oldest poured concrete structures in the region.

### Wood Preserving Plant
Santa Fe RR Right of Way
Las Vegas vicinity

The Santa Fe RR built this plant, where wood was treated with preservatives for use as ties, bridge timbers, etc. In operation

from 1885–1925, the site today is an unmarked ruin.

### Illinois Brewery
Neal Avenue and 6th Street
Socorro (UTM: 13.325550.3770540)

The site includes an ice maker, boiler, ammonia condenser and a water tank. The brewery opened in 1882 and erected a stone building in 1886 to replace an earlier adobe structure. The concern, closed by Prohibition, never reopened.

### Laureano Cordova Mill
near State Route 75
Vadito vicinity

The Cordova mill, a horizontal gristmill run by water power, is similar to the earliest mills in the Southwest. Built ca. 1870, it is

still used seasonally. Grain is milled between grindstones.

## NEW YORK

### Brooklyn Bridge
Adams Street at East River
Brooklyn (UTM: 18.584790.4506300)

Sixteen years in the making, the bridge was designed and built by John Roebling and his son, and completed in 1883. For twenty years it was the longest bridge in the U.S., at 1,595 feet. Roebling pioneered the use of clustered wires in the main cables.

### Motion Picture Film Warehouse
Vitagraph Company, Inc.
791 East 43rd Street
Brooklyn (UTM: 18.589980.4498680)

The warehouse, owned by Warner Bros.

137

Pictures, employs an elaborate ventilation system, necessitated by the fact that, when the warehouse was built, around 1925, the movie film it was to store was highly flammable and produced lethal fumes when it burned. The warehouse is still in use; it holds about 3 million feet of film.

### Electric Grain Elevator
Buffalo

Of the dozens of grain elevators built at Buffalo since the 1840s, 15 remain. The most interesting of them may be this all-steel structure, built in 1897, which was the first Buffalo elevator to use the new hydroelectric power from Niagara Falls.

### Pierce-Arrow Factory Complex
Elmwood and Great Arrow Avenues
Buffalo (UTM: 17.673120.4756640)

Built in 1906 to a design by Albert Kahn, the factories occupy a 34-acre site and comprise 14 major buildings, including the Administration Building (reinforced concrete with brick and steel sides) and an Assembly Building (of the same material, with a saw-tooth roof, planned to admit sunlight).

### Water Turbines
Harmony Mill No. 3
100 North Mohawk Street
Cohoes (UTM: 18.605970.4737050)

Probably the largest hydraulic turbines in the U.S., these two are 102-inch Boyden-type devices, rated at 800 horsepower each. They were installed ca. 1872 to drive the machinery in the Harmony mill.

### West Point Foundry
State Route 9D
Cold Spring vicinity

A dilapidated office building, ca. 1865, is the only relic of what was once the largest iron foundry in the U.S. Established in 1817, the works produced cannon, steam engines, ironclad shipping (including the *Merrimac*) and the Dewitt Clinton locomotive.

### New Croton Dam
Croton Dam Road
Cortland (UTM: 18.595900.4564280)

The masonry dam was built between 1892–1906 as the principal dam in the Croton system, which provides water for New York City. It is 1,168 feet long and 291 feet high, with hewn granite facing.

### Elevated Watch Tower
Central Avenue
Cortland

The two-story steel tower, bearing on a concrete foundation, was raised in 1850 as part of the Erie Lackawanna RR line in the re-

Paterson Silk Machinery Exchange building, New Jersey

gion. The watch house atop the tower is wood.

### Lord and Burnham Factory
2 Main Street
Irvington

The factory opened in 1870 for the manufacture of greenhouses. The firm built some of the first iron-frame greenhouses in the U.S., for Jay Gould's estate at Lyndhurst. The factory is still in operation (access by permission).

### Gladden-Milks Windmill
Pigeon Valley Road
Napoli (UTM: 17.673640.4677820)

The wind turbine is adjusted by movable shutters surrounding the rotor. Mill machinery is housed in a three-story frame building. Built in 1890, the mill is deteriorating.

### Bridle Path Arch Bridge
Central Park near 96th Street
New York

Built in 1869, the cast-iron bridge, now in a deteriorated condition, has gothic motifs. It has been closed to pedestrian traffic.

### Cooper Union
Seventh Street and 4th Avenue
New York (UTM: 18.585220.4509000)

Built in 1859 to provide higher education for the city's poor, the construction uses wrought-iron beams as weight-bearers on a scale that was at the time an innovation in building technology.

### Municipal Asphalt Plant
York Avenue and 90th Street
New York

Asphalt making equipment is housed in an unusual building constructed of four reinforced concrete parabolic arches. The plant building, built in 1944, was designed by Kahn & Jacobs, architects.

### Pier A
Battery Place at Hudson River
New York (UTM: 18.582940.4506180)

City Pier A was built in 1886 to house the New York Dock Department and the harbor police. The two-story rectangular building was enlarged in 1900 and again in 1904.

### Curtis Steam Turbine
General Electric Plant
Schenectady

The 5,000-kilowatt turbine generator, built in 1903 by GE, was the most powerful steam turbine in the world. The shaft is vertical, and the electric generator was mounted above the turbine.

### Cast-Iron Storehouse
Watervliet Arsenal
Westervelt Avenue at Gibson Street
Watervliet (UTM: 18.606080.4730120)

The arsenal, built in 1859, may be the only early all-iron building still used for its original purpose. All components, outside and inside, were prefabricated at a New York City iron works. Access is restricted.

Union Station, Indianapolis

139

140

West Baden Hotel, French Lick, Indiana

## NORTH CAROLINA

### McKay Farm Machinery Factory
Railroad Avenue
Dunn

The site includes three frame buildings in which the McKay firm, still in operation, has made farm implements since 1895. The buildings are: an assembly/shipping house, a machine shop, and a foundry.

### Bull Durham Tobacco Factory
Pettigrew Street
Durham (UTM: 17.688900.3985100)

The ornate Victorian-Italianate factory was raised in 1875 and added to some ten years later. Behind its sumptuous exterior, the factory has a notably efficient and well-planned layout.

### Glencoe Cotton Mills
State Route 1600
Glencoe (UTM: 17.641420.4000240)

A well-preserved mill village, Glencoe was organized in 1882. Brick mill buildings, finishing mill and warehouses survive, as well as wood-frame mill workers' housing and a water turbine with some related machinery.

### Ceramic Pipe Works
Pamona Terra Cotta Manufacturing
  Company
West Market Street
Greensboro (UTM: 17.602100.3991280)

The site includes about 30 beehive kilns, each 15–20 feet high, in which clay pipe—used as sanitary sewer pipe—is fired. The works opened in 1886. Beehive kilns are now being replaced by kilns of a more efficient design.

### Seaboard Coast Line RR Depot
Main Street
Hamlet (UTM: 17.618920.3860730)

The passenger depot was built in 1900 as a two-story frame building, L-shaped, with a large projecting pavilion at the outer angle of the L. There have been extensive additions and alterations, but the main waiting room remains essentially unchanged.

### North State Mining Company
Copper Branch
Jamestown vicinity
  (UTM: 17.596660.3980060)

The site contains a ruined building of dry-wall random hewn granite stones about 40 feet high with a 60-foot chimney. The building may have been the smelter for a gold mining company known to have operated in the region ca. 1832.

### McAden Cotton Mills
Main Street
McAdenville (UTM: 17.493060.3901580)

The mills opened in 1881, running on water power. Three buildings, all brick, one a large towered structure, comprise the site.

### Mount Airy Furniture Co.
Mount Airy and Factory Streets
Mount Airy (UTM: 17.535300.4038540)

The company was organized in 1896, also the date of the factory building, a long, two-story frame structure. The firm is still in business, manufacturing bedroom furniture.

### Atlantic Coast Line RR Pumping Station
Nashville and Hammond Streets
Rocky Mount

The one-story brick building and 60-foot-high water tank were built ca. 1920 to serve the Atlantic Coast Line's repair shops. Abandoned in the mid-1950s, the station has been taken over for use as an arts center.

### Southern RR Shops
Salisbury Avenue
Spencer (UTM: 17.551100.3949120)

The complex was begun in 1896, and soon became the principal repair shop of the Southern RR. A large machine shop (1905), a 37-stall roundhouse (1925), and other buildings today stand deserted.

### J. C. Steele & Sons
Mulberry Street and Steele Street
Statesville (UTM: 17.509980.3958820)

Steele made bricks here beginning after the Civil War; after 1889 he turned to manufacturing brick-making machinery, still the business of the firm. The oldest building on the site is the old brick works, a brick building with a gabled roof, from which the old cupola furnace has been removed.

### Tarboro Cotton Press
Albemarle and Wilson Streets
Tarboro

Originally used for producing cider and wine, the 22-foot-high pine structure was built ca. 1840, and used to bale cotton from ca. 1860. It was driven by mules.

### Shell Service Station
Peachtree and Sprague Streets
Winston-Salem (UTM: 17.570780.3990520)

A local distributor of Shell oil products built this stucco and concrete station in the shape of a scallop shell ca. 1930. It was one of three in the area, and is the only one that survives. The unusual building is a lawnmower repair shop at present.

## NORTH DAKOTA

### Fargo & Southern RR Depot
1101 Second Avenue North
Fargo (UTM: 14.667960.5193835)

Built to impress in 1884, the two-story depot failed to ensure the success of the Fargo & Southern, and was soon taken over by the Milwaukee Road Line. The gable roof is wood-framed and was originally covered with lead or copper roofing.

### Eastwood Park Bridge
Central Avenue and 6th Street, S.E.
Minot (UTM: 14.330392.5344853)

A cantilever T-beam bridge of concrete, three-span, completed in 1927 and extensively altered in 1946.

## OHIO

### Goodyear Airdock
Akron Airport
Akron (UTM: 17.460420.4542200)

The building was built in 1929 by the Goodyear Zeppelin Corp., which made dirigibles there. The building is made of sheet metal attached to 11 parabolic arches; it is 1,175 feet long, 211 feet high and 325 feet across. At each end is a door that weighs 600 tons. These open and close by means of a system of rollers and rails.

### D. Picking & Company
119 South Walnut Street
Bucyrus

The firm makes hand-hammered copper kettles, the same product, made in much the same ways, that it has been making since 1874. The factory building is essentially unchanged.

### Stone Bridge
Old U.S. Route 40
Cambridge

The bridge is of sandstone ashlar. It has a 45-foot span comprising a single segmental arch.

### Cincinnati Union Terminal
1301 Western Avenue
Cincinnati

Built between 1929–33, this is one of the last large-scale RR stations to be built in the U.S. It is in an Art-Deco architectural style, and includes monumental mosaic murals within.

### Pumping Station
Cincinnati Water Works
Route 52 at Ohio River
Cincinnati

The site includes a circular, two-story masonry engine house in the Romanesque Revival style (ca. 1908) that houses four Corliss triple-expansion vertical pumping engines.

### Pumping Station
Division Avenue at 45th Street
Cleveland

The five-story brick station houses three vertical, triple-expansion, crank-and-flywheel steam pumps. The engines were built between 1914–17 by Allis Chalmers. Each flywheel is 20 feet in diameter and weighs 30 tons.

### Central RR Station
379 West Broad Street
Columbus

The Toledo & Ohio Central RR built this station in 1895, five years before the line was absorbed by another railroad. The brown brick, two-story depot has octagonal wings and a central tower "of Oriental inspiration."

### Nela Park
1901 Noble Road
East Cleveland (UTM: 17.453200.4598800)

Perhaps the first planned industrial park in

141

the U.S., the complex was built by the National Electric Lamp Association (NELA) between 1911 and 1921. The site includes 20 major buildings, most of them in the Georgian Revival style, on a landscaped park-like campus.

### Pottery Factory
Second and Market Streets
East Liverpool

The upright or "bottle" kiln on the site, used for the firing of yellow brick and Rockingham pottery ware, is one of the oldest kilns of its type in the U.S. Pottery making started on the site ca. 1844.

### Harding-Jones Paper Company District
3651 South Main Street
Excello (UTM: 16.721880.4372580)

The site includes a brick paper mill (1871), two residences, a carriage house and a canal lock of the Miami & Erie Canal. The factory, which has been successively powered by water, steam and electricity, is still in operation; some late-1800s machinery is still in use.

### Fairport Lighthouse Museum
Second Street
Fairport Harbor

The lighthouse and adjacent keeper's house were built in 1871, replacing earlier structures (1825). The lighthouse was decommissioned in 1925 and now houses the only Great Lakes lighthouse museum.

### Germantown Covered Bridge
Germantown

A rare inverted bow-string truss. Built in 1870, the 103-foot bridge was moved from its original site on the Dayton Pike to the present location in 1911.

### Buckeye Furnace
Jackson vicinity
(UTM: 17.373900.4323850)

The site includes storage sheds, a furnace, and a casting house where molten iron was cast into pigs. In operation from ca. 1850, the complex has been extensively restored by the state.

### Kent Industrial District
Main, River and Franklin Streets
Kent

The district includes five structures on a tract on both sides of the Cuyahoga River. There are: a three-arch masonry bridge (ca. 1885); a concave stone dam (late 1830s); a brick RR depot; a five-story brick-and-stone cotton mill (ca. 1851); and a brick livery stable (ca. 1910).

### Peninsula Village Historic District
State Route 303
Peninsula

The site preserves intact what was from 1827–87 a thriving canal and mercantile town. Gristmills, boat yards, and sandstone quarries contributed to Peninsulas' prosperity when it was a busy stop on the Ohio Canal (Akron to Cleveland).

### Piqua Historical Area
State Route 66
Piqua

The Miami and Erie Canal, dug between 1825–45, ran 248 miles from Toledo to Cincinnati. At Piqua there are a lock, turning basins, and a replica of the *General Harrison,* a cargo boat of ca. 1840–50.

## OKLAHOMA

### Jenson RR Tunnel
Off State Route 112
Cameron vicinity

Built in 1886 by the Fort Smith & Southern RR, this is the only RR tunnel in the state. It is 1,180 feet long and still in use.

### Nida Cotton Gin
Nida

Cotton production began to thrive in Oklahoma about 1900 and reached its peak ca. 1920, when 700–800 gins were in operation. Three hundred remain, of which this one (built in 1930) is typical.

### Santa Fe RR Depot
Main Street and Minnesota Avenue
Shawnee

The castle-like depot, built in 1903, is of red sandstone with a hip roof, dome and tower. It is probably the most striking RR building in Oklahoma.

### Slaughter House
Stillwater vicinity

The first slaughter house in the area; much equipment still in place.

### Golda's Mill
State Route 51
Stillwell vicinity

Of the original mill building (ca. 1838) little remains, though the original overshot waterwheel and milling machinery (from the 1830s) remain in use in a restored building.

### Pennington Creek Bridge
Tishomingo vicinity

The cable anchors of the suspension bridge are deteriorated, though it is still in use by autos.

### Union RR Depot
Tulsa

Built around 1910, the station is an unusually large specimen.

### Old Faucet Oil Well
Wapanucka vicinity

Only the head of a 6-inch casing remains

Heavy gear machinery, Thomas Kay Woolen Mill

Thomas Kay Woolen Mill, Salem, Oregon

to mark the site of Oklahoma's first successful oil well, drilled in 1885 and abandoned three years later.

## OREGON

### Elmore Salmon Cannery
Flaval Street
Astoria

The plant was built in 1881 and is the oldest salmon cannery still in use in the U.S. An old bunkhouse that housed Chinese laborers is also on the site.

### Logging Museum
Collier State Park
Route 97
Klamath Falls vicinity

The museum's collection includes old saws, high-wheels, donkey engines, and surveying and scaling instruments.

### Oregon Iron Company Furnace
George Rogers Park
Lake Oswego

The first pig iron produced west of the Rockies came from the basalt blast furnace at Lake Oswego in 1867. The furnace had a capacity of eight tons of iron per day, and produced the iron for many of the cast-iron building facades of Portland.

### Willamette Falls Locks
West Linn
Oregon City

The complex comprises five locks, which vary in depth from 19–40 feet, and achieve a total vertical lift of 41–50 feet. The locks, built in 1873, are of native stone.

### Thomas Kay Woolen Mill
260 Twelfth Street, S.W.
Salem

The timber-frame and brick mill, built in 1896, was modeled on similar mills on the Atlantic seaboard. Today it can still be run by the old direct-drive water power system. A dye house, office buildings, water tank and boiler room are among the outbuildings on the site.

## PENNSYLVANIA

### Tannery
Bethlehem Historic Subdivision A
Bethlehem (UTM: 18.467470.4496440)

The massive limestone tannery, in operation from 1761 to 1870, was strategically located adjacent to the community's butchershop and stockyards. A nearby mill ground tanbark. Original vat bases survive; vats have been restored, together with chimneys and other parts of the structure.

### Hopewell Village Historic Site
Birdsboro vicinity

The community grew up around a charcoal-burning blast furnace that opened in 1743 and operated for 140 years, supplying iron for the American Revolution as well as stoves, pots and pans, and machinery. The furnace's production peaked in 1853.

### Columbia Market House
Third and Main Streets
Columbia

The market house, which dates from 1850–70, is a rectilinear brick structure, about 80-by-300 feet. The roof is supported by arched wooden lattice trusses and wrought-iron tie rods.

### Coplay Cement Kilns
North Main Street
Coplay

The first portland cement in the U.S. reputedly came from these vertical cement kilns (1875), the only remaining vertical kilns in the country. The company was founded in 1866. The portland cement kilns have been disused since ca. 1900.

### Mercer Museum
Pine and Ashland Streets
Doylestown

The museum has one of the largest collections of tools, machines and similar implements in the world (30,000 items). The building itself (1916) is noteworthy, too—a castle-like structure built entirely of reinforced concrete, down to the floors, window frames and roof.

### Moravian Tile and Pottery Works
Court Street and Swamp Road
Doylestown

Built in 1912, the reinforced concrete factory, laid out around an open courtyard, contains five kilns. It is open as a museum.

### Allegheny Portage RR Route and
###    Pennsylvania Canal
U.S. Route 22
Johnstown

This National Historic Site includes portions of the Allegheny Portage line (built 1831–4); the first RR tunnel in the U.S. (1831–4); and the stone foundations of the engine house at the head of one of the canal's inclined planes.

### Johnstown Incline Railway
Johns Street and Edgehill Drive
Johnstown

The railway was built in 1890–1 by the Cambria Iron Co. to provide transportation (in two cable-driven cars) for workers to a company housing development, Westmont. The 986-foot-long incline was one of the longest and steepest in the world, and is today one of the last surviving systems of its kind. Originally powered by steam, the railway is run today as a tourist attraction, powered by an electric motor.

**Manyunk Mill District**
Mail and Lock Streets
Manyunk

Many old textile mills survive in this village on the Schuylkill River.

**Fairmont Water Works**
Fairmont Park
Philadelphia

Philadelphia's municipal water system was the first in the U.S. to use steam-powered pumps. Begun in 1799, the system added steam pumps to the Fairmont station in 1822. The steam plant continued to operate until 1911, and much of the old machinery is still in place.

**Philadelphia Gas Works**
Passyunk Avenue
Philadelphia

The works opened in 1854 with four retort houses, a pumphouse, a meter house and what was then the world's largest gasholder. Major alterations were carried out late in the last century, but several of the old structures remain in use today.

**Union RR Station and Rotunda**
1101 Liberty Avenue
Pittsburgh

The Pennsylvania RR built the magnificent turreted rotunda with its four centered arches, as well as the 12-story office structure in a Beaux Arts style, in 1898–1903.

**Westinghouse Atom Smasher**
Forest Hills
Pittsburgh

When it was built in 1937, the Westinghouse installation was the world's largest nuclear physics research plant. The center housed a generator and a 40-foot vacuum tube. The atom smasher was decommissioned in 1958.

**Drake Oil Well**
Drake Well Park
State Route 27
Titusville vicinity

The first oil well in the world (1859). The derrick and associated structures have been restored.

**Brother's Furniture Store**
Main Street
Tremont

The store has its original stamped tin facade, a late-nineteenth-century survival, preserved in good condition.

## RHODE ISLAND

**Arnold's Mills**
Route 120 near Route 114
Cumberland (UTM: 19.301700.4650020)

The two-story wood building was built in 1825 and housed a machine shop that made cotton machinery and spinning frames until about 1870, when it was used as a straw hat factory and blacksmith shop. From 1912

into the 1960s, a gristmill was housed in the building.

**Grants Mills**
Route 121 at Route 114
Cumberland (UTM: 19.299820.4653240)

This combination saw- and gristmill was built about 1818, though the earliest dated machinery is from midcentury. The water-driven apparatus, including a reciprocating saw, remains in place. The mill closed in 1932, and is now being restored.

**Bridge Mill Power Plant**
Main Street at Main Street Bridge
Pawtucket (UTM: 19.302140.4638580)

The brick electric generating station was built in 1893–4, and could run on steam or water power. The five pairs of 33-inch McCormick turbines are still in place, though the old steam engines and boilers have been removed. The plant last produced power in the 1960s.

**Old Slater Mill**
Roosevelt Avenue
Pawtucket (UTM: 19.302220.4638700)

This is the first successful cotton textile factory in North America to use Arkwright's system of water-frame spinning. Wood-frame, 2½ stories high, it was built in 1793 and has been added to extensively since. In 1832 the mill contained 2,300 spindles and 48 looms, and employed 90 workers. Since

Ichabod Williams Veneer Plant, Carteret, New Jersey

1955 the building has been used as a museum.

**Wilkinson Mill**
Roosevelt Avenue at Main Street
Pawtucket (UTM: 19.302220.4638700)
Built in 1810–11, the 3½-story stone mill is a very early example of the stone textile mills that later became common in the region. Between 1810–29 the owner, David Wilkinson, developed an early power loom on this site.

**Lippitt Mill**
825 Main Street
West Warwick
Still in operation, the mill has produced cotton textiles since 1810. It is a rare survivor of the early wood-frame mills, many of which have burned.

**Woonsocket Mills No. 1 and No. 2**
110 and 115 Front Street
Woonsocket
Built in 1829 and 1833, respectively, the two mills are fine examples of early New England cotton textile factories. No. 2 is distinguished by its handsome proportions and Greek Revival detailing. It is still in partial use, for woolen weaving.

# SOUTH CAROLINA

**Northeastern RR Warehouse**
2 Chapel Street
Charleston
The warehouse, built in 1881, was one of a pair of RR buildings in the fanciful "Chinese" style of the Victorian period.

**Powder Magazine**
79 Cumberland Street
Charleston
The low, square magazine, of stuccoed brick with a four-sided pyramidal roof, was built in 1713. It was used to store gunpowder until ca. 1783.

**Georgetown Lighthouse**
North Island
Georgetown (UTM: 17.668880.3677220)
Built in 1801 and rebuilt in 1812 and 1867, the 87-foot tower is brick, while inside the stairs and center posts are stone. The light is still in use and is maintained by the Coast Guard.

**McBee Mill**
Reedy River Falls Historic Park
Greenville
The site includes the ruins of a brick and grante gristmill built in the 1830s.

**Paul Pritchard Shipyard**
Hobcaw Creek
Mt. Pleasant vicinity
  (UTM: 17.605130.3632230)
In operation by 1702, the yard was acquired by Pritchard in 1778 and used during the Revolution for converting merchant ships into warships. Sold for debt in 1831, the yard never reopened.

# SOUTH DAKOTA

**Lead Historic District**
Lead (UTM: 13.599360.4911800)
Settled in 1876, Lead is a gold-mining town associated with the Homestake Mining Co. The buildings, generally simple structures, are built along the sides of the Black Hills.

**Rock Island RR Depot**
210 East 10th Street
Sioux Falls
Constructed in 1885, the Romanesque Revival depot is of stone with a hipped roof and an octagonal turret. It has been disused since 1970.

**Bon Homme Mill**
Gavins Point Reservoir
Tabor vicinity
Built in 1875 by a colony of Hutterian Brethren, the gristmill is of chalk stone, 2½ story, with clapboard gables.

# TENNESSEE

**Big Bone Saltpeter Mine**
Bone Cave vicinity
Saltpeter (potassium nitrate), an ingredient of gunpowder, was mined here extensively during the War of 1812, and again during the Civil War. During the Civil War, an elevated tramway was erected at the site.

**Gas Works**
Clarksville Industrial District
Union and Washington Streets
Clarksville
The one-story brick gas works (1870s) housed gas generating equipment for the city system. The gasholder is gone.

**Grange Warehouse**
Clarksville Industrial District
Washington Street
Clarksville
The red brick, three-story warehouse was built in 1859 to house a planing mill, but has always been used as a tobacco warehouse. It is in good condition, but has been altered extensively.

**RR Freight Station**
Clarksville Industrial District
Adams Street
Clarksville
The Louisville & Nashville built this station, notable for its handsome brick-arched loading portals, in 1898.

**RR Trestle and Bridge**
Clarksville Industrial District
Crossland Avenue
Clarksville
The elaborate and intricate timber trestle, and the Parker truss bridge, were built ca. 1901 by the local Tennessee Central RR.

**Swing RR Bridge**
Clarksville Industrial District
Adams Street
Clarksville
Built ca. 1859 by the Louisville & Nash-ville RR, the bridge has three spans, and is 678 feet long and 51 feet high. The center span swings open to permit shipping to pass.

**Casey Jones Home and Museum**
211 West Chester Street
Jackson
The chief interest of the site is in a ten-wheeler locomotive of the type (ca. 1900) driven by Casey.

**Second Avenue Commercial District**
2nd Avenue North
Nashville
The area has one of the outstanding American collections of cast-iron and masonry storefronts. The buildings, most of which are three or four stories high and a full block deep, date from the 1870s and '80s.

**Pigeon Forge Mill**
Pigeon River
Pigeon Forge (UTM: 17.269160.3963300)
The site includes a gristmill built in 1830. Power came from a large mill dam, which drove a 24-foot breast wheel. At one time an iron forge, looms, and a sawmill were also on the site.

**Readyville Mill**
Readyville
The five-story gristmill, of heavy-timber construction with wood clapboard siding, was built in the late 1860s and contains working milling machinery of the period.

**Arthur Pitt Home and Distillery**
Highway 49
Springfield
Three buildings survive on the site: a residence, warehouse, and distillery. All are timber and clapboard. The distillery operated from ca. 1800 to 1909.

# TEXAS

**J. S. Cullinan Refinery**
Mobil Petroleum Park
Corsicana
The oil refinery was built in 1898, and became the first successful refinery in the Southwest. Today it is largely in ruins.

**Galveston Bagging and Cordage Company Factory**
Winnie Street at 38th Street
Galveston
Woven jute bagging, used to cover cotton bales, was made here beginning in 1888. The plant was run by steam, and the brick building had an early cistern-and-sprinkler system for fire fighting.

**Gruene Historic District**
Gruene (UTM: 14.586650.3289960)
The village grew up in ca. 1872 as a cotton producing community. On the site are: homes, a cotton gin (originally water powered), two stores, a boiler house, and a 100-foot water tower (ca. 1920). Gruene began to decline in the 1920s, when cotton crops were ravaged by the boll weevil.

Tredegar Iron Works, Richmond

**Alamo Roman and Portland Cement Company**
Brackenridge Park
San Antonio

Remains include foundation and walls (coursed limestone rubble), and a chimney ringed with iron reinforcing hoops. The firm, an early western maker of portland cement, was organized in 1880.

**Menger Soap Works**
North Laredo Street
San Antonio

The soap factory opened in 1850. It is built of limestone blocks and rubble. Operations ceased early in this century. The building has been converted into apartments.

**Suspension Bridge**
Bridge Street
Waco (UTM: 14.677790.3493100)

The wire-cable, single-span suspension bridge, 475 feet long, crosses the Brazos River at a height of 57 feet. Built in 1870, it has stuccoed brick cable towers. The original stiffening trusses were wood. The span is now used as a foot bridge.

## UTAH

**Oil Shale Retort**
Willow Creek
Agency Draw vicinity

The basic structure of the retort and the walls of a stone building are all that remain on the site. The retort, built in 1922 to extract oil from shale, could process 10 tons of shale (= 10 barrels of oil) per day The retort was never put in commercial production, and ran only for about a year.

**Old Irontown**
Cedar City vicinity

The site includes remains of an iron-mining complex that functioned from 1868–76. The deposits were discovered in 1849, and the workings began in 1851–2.

**Olmstead Station Power House**
U.S. Highway 189
Provo Canyon

The station was built in 1903. The Telluride Institute, a pioneer in electrical engineering education, was on the site.

**Open Pit Copper Mine**
Bingham Canyon
Salt Lake City vicinity

Seventeen percent of all U.S. copper comes from here. The mine, which is 1½ miles across and ½ mile deep, was opened in 1904.

**Union Pacific RR Station**
South Temple Street
Salt Lake City
   (UTM: 12.423840.4513350)

The station (1908–9) has a central waiting room with wings to each side. The central area is 100 by 36 feet. Walls are of cut grey sandstone fronting reinforced concrete. Upper walls are brick. The depot's most notable feature is its huge black slate mansard roof, complete with entablatures and crestwork in the French Second Empire style.

**Z.C.M.I. Store Front**
15 South Main Street
Salt Lake City

The Zion Cooperative Mercantile Institute built this, one of the first department stores in the U.S., in 1876. The store, which has an unusually well preserved cast-iron front, has 50 feet of street frontage and is 318 feet deep.

## VERMONT

**Estey Organ Factories**
Birge Street
Brattleboro

The Estey firm made organs of all sizes in this complex of buildings, which date from about 1870. The factories are remarkable in that slate shingles cover the entire buildings, not the roofs only. Today some of the surviving factory buildings are used for storage, or for discount stores.

**Pontoon Bridge**
Brookfield Village

The 320-foot floating bridge, one of the last in the east, was built in 1936. It is made of heavy timbers with metal splices at the joints and a plank deck. It floats on 380 fifty-gallon barrels chained to its understructure.

**Murdock Woolen Mill**
State Route 131
Proctorsville

Built in 1845, the building is a three-story structure with an attic pierced by clerestory windows. Construction is brick with granite trim. The whole is similar to the mills of Harrisville, New Hampshire.

**Central Vermont RR Complex**
Allen Street
St. Albans

The site includes 12 buildings built between 1865 and 1923. The depot, considered by many students to be the finest in New England, was destroyed in 1963. Remaining structures include a mansard-roofed office building, shops, and switch house. All are of brick.

**Sidewheel Steamboat** *Ticonderoga*
Shelburne Museum

Shelburne

The *Ticonderoga* was launched in 1906 and plied Lake Champlain until 1954. It is 220 feet long, has a steel hull, and is driven by two 25-foot paddlewheels mounted amidships on either side. A walking-beam steam engine drives the wheels.

### Ascutney Mill Dam
Windsor (UTM: 18.7107.48168)

This gravity-arch dam was built in 1834; it is one of the few surviving large dams built before 1850. The dam is apparently rubble filled. Its exterior is of cut granite. Total length is 360 feet; and maximum height is 40 feet.

## VIRGINIA

### White's Gristmill
Abingdon vicinity

Built in the mid-nineteenth century, and operated exclusively by water power to the present, the two-story frame mill is driven by an overshot waterwheel. A buhr stone, roller milling equipment, and bolting/sifting machinery, are all in place. All interior gears and works (except the main gear wheel) are handmade of wood.

### Bellona Arsenal
Midlothian vicinity

Established in 1814, the arsenal supplied the U.S., then the Confederacy. The site consisted of the main arsenal, officer's quarters, workshops, a barracks and a powder magazine. The last survives with three workshops.

### Petersburg Gas Light Company Gasholder
Madison and Bank Streets
Petersburg (UTM: 18.287340.4123030)

The iron gasholder, one of 12 when it was installed in 1851–2, is 60 feet across and 40 feet high. It is supported by six double sets of decorative cast-iron columns.

### Drydock No. 1
Naval Shipyard
Portsmouth

Built as part of a naval program authorized by Congress in 1827, the drydock was finished in 1834 and is still in use. It is constructed of large blocks of Massachusetts granite, and is 319 feet long.

### Tredegar Iron Works
James River and Kanawha Canal
Richmond (UTM: 18.283790.4156850)

Chartered in 1837, the Tredegar works were in full swing by the 1850s, and remained one of America's most important iron works through the Civil War. The plant survived the war but declined after the financial panic of 1873. The site is now in ruins.

### Cyrus McCormick House and Workshop
Staunton vicinity

McCormick produced the first mechanical reaper here in 1831. A blacksmith shop, farmhouse and gristmill remain.

## WASHINGTON

### Blewett Arrastra
Route 97 at Culver Gulch
Chelan County

An arrastra is a quartz-crusher. Most arrastras were powered by animals, and worked like stone gristmills. This one, built in 1860 and in use until 1880, was water powered. It is cut into bedrock on its site.

### Curtis Steam Turbines
Seattle Department of Lighting
Seattle

Installed in 1906 to run generators for the city electric system, two of the 3,000-kilowatt vertical turbines are still maintained for emergency use.

### Lake Station Gasworks
Meridian Avenue North
Seattle

The station was established in 1906 to produce retort and carbureted water gas, converted to oil-gas production in 1937, and closed in the mid-1950s when the Seattle gas system was converted to natural gas.

### Lake Washington Ship Canal and Locks
Seattle

The canal system was begun in 1911 and finished in 1917. It connects Puget Sound with a fresh-water harbor area that includes Lake Washington. The complex has a spillway dam and two locks.

### Union Passenger Station
1713 Pacific Avenue
Tacoma

The depot was the end of the Northern Pacific RR's line. Designed (1910) by the architects of New York's Grand Central Terminal, the Tacoma station is a large dome resting on four vaults. The building is surmounted by a copper dome.

## WEST VIRGINA

### Baltimore & Ohio RR Roundhouse
Race and Martin Streets
Martinsburg (UTM: 18.245300.4371650)

Built in 1866 to replace an earlier structure that had been destroyed by Confederate troops, the West Roundhouse was notable for its cast-iron structural frame and intricate cast-iron strut construction. It was turned to other uses after 1913.

### Potomac Edison Company Hydroelectric
    Station
Potomac River
Shepherdstown (UTM: 18.256920.4375280)

The 1,000-kilowatt station is run by turbines driven by dammed water. The generators are unusual in that they are connected to the turbines by ropes. This system of drive-transfer, common in the early 1900s when the plant was built (1908–9), may survive nowhere else today.

### LaBelle Works
31st Street and Wood Street
Wheeling

The factory made cut nails. Established in 1852, it was converted to cannon manufacture for a period.

## WISCONSIN

### Cedarburg Mill
215 East Columbia Avenue
Cedarburg

Built in 1855, the five-story gray limestone mill was capable of producing 120 barrels of flour per day. Currently the building is used as a warehouse.

### Chambers Island Lighthouse
Chambers Island
Gibraltar vicinity
    (UTM: 16.471300.5005250)

The lighthouse and keeper's quarters are a 1½-story brick building with a three-story octagonal light tower. Built in 1868, the station is no longer used and the light has been removed. A new automatic light installation stands in an enclosure near the site.

### Iron Block
205 East Wisconsin Avenue
Milwaukee

The building (1861) is a narrow rectangular structure with cast-iron construction on two elevations. The framing is conventional brick-and-timber, with inverted semicircular brick arches as the foundations of the cast-iron walls.

### Metropolitan Sewage Treatment Plant
Milwaukee

The plant opened in 1919 and was one of the country's first large-scale activated-sludge-type municipal treatment facility.

### Kehl Winery
State Route 188
Prairie du Sac vicinity
    (UTM: 16.280350.4796230)

The vineyards and winery were first founded in 1857. The site includes a limestone-lined cave or tunnel as a wine cellar, a limestone-block-and-rubble winery, and a residence. The operation continued in production until 1899, when frost destroyed the vines.

### Jung Carriage Factory
829–35 Pennsylvania Avenue
Sheboygan

The factory, built ca. 1885–7, built carriages, wagons and sleighs. The building is of timber and brick construction with molded masonry details and iron ornamentation on the facade.

## WYOMING

### Piedmont Charcoal Kilns
Hilliard vicinity

The site, which included 40 kilns, produced charcoal for use by nearby mine smelters. The first kilns were built in 1869. Three remain. Made of native sandstone, the conical kilns are about 30 feet high and have 8-foot-high entrance ports.

# Bibliographical Essay

A number of books on industrial archeology have appeared in the past ten years, most in Great Britain, dealing with British sites. In my opinion, the best of these, and the one that offers the most helpful introduction to the subject, is R. A. Buchanan's *Industrial Archaeology in Britain*, published as a paperback by Penguin Books Ltd., in 1972 and recently reissued in a revised edition. Another British work of interest for American readers is Kenneth Hudson's *Exploring Our Industrial Past* (Hodder & Stoughton, 1975), which argues persuasively for understanding the lives of the people who made up the nineteenth century's industrial working population, and the ways in which industry was shaped by the workers and they by it. *The Techniques of Industrial Archaeology* by J. P. M. Pannell (edited by Kenneth Major, David & Charles, 1974), gives the ABC's of field work and should be supplemented with Harley J. McKee's good *Recording Historic Buildings* (U.S. Government Printing Office, 1970). For a comprehensive bibliography of writings on American industry in the beginning years see Brooke Hindle's *Technology in Early America* (University of North Carolina Press, 1966). An overview of developments in New England prior to the Civil War is provided by Dirk J. Struik in *Yankee Science in the Making* (Collier Books, 1968). Carl W. Condit's *American Building* (University of Chicago Press, 1968) is a useful survey of building materials and methods.

Other sources that are musts for North American industrial archeologists include: *Technology and Culture*, the international quarterly of the Society for the History of Technology, published by the University of Chicago Press; the Smithsonian Institution's Studies in History and Technology series, which includes *A Report of the Mohawk–Hudson Area Survey*, conducted in 1969 by the Historic American Engineering Record, and edited by Robert M. Vogel in 1973; the inventory catalogs published by the Historic American Engineering Record, giving extensive listings of historic engineering and industrial sites by individual states (the most recently issued are those for Delaware and North Carolina); and lastly, the Society for Industrial Archeology's periodicals. The *SIA Newsletter* is published ten times a year and contains a great deal of current information on work in progress, future meetings of the Society and related organizations, as well as up-to-date reports on new books, articles and reprints of interest. This is complemented by *IA*, a journal, which appears twice annually and has scholarly articles, detailed field reports, and book reviews.

There are also many good books on specific aspects of industry or technology, such as Ross Holland, Jr.'s *America's Lighthouses* (The Stephen Greene Press, 1972), and others that you'll discover as your interest in a particular industry deepens and you begin to delve further on your own.

# Acknowledgments

This book has taken far longer to write than it took to build most of the structures included in it, and could not have been written at all without the full support and co-operation of a number of persons. I am especially indebted to Steve and Jan Greene for their inspiration, patience, and good advice. Robert M. Vogel, Curator of Mechanical and Civil Engineering at The Smithsonian Institution, and Eric N. Delony, Principal Architect of the Historic American Engineering Record, have given far more generously of time and constructive thought in reviewing drafts than one has a right to expect. R. Carole Huberman was helpful in gathering material during the early stages; Peter Stott calculated the UTM co-ordinates, where possible, as well as explanatory material. Williams College's Class of 1900 Fund provided support for my own research and for preparation of the initial typescript while I was a member of the faculty there. As this is mainly a photograhic essay, it owes much to the excellent camera work and sincere interest of Jack Boucher, whose unselfishness and high professionalism is deeply appreciated. Thanks are due also to Wm. Barrett and Allan Seymour for their good photographs. Robert L. Dothard has been a sympathetic and helpful designer, and Castle Freeman, Jr., and Walter Hard, Jr., have been equally candid and creative editors—not an easy task when dealing with someone who always seemed to want to say whatever it was more stodgily than they thought palatable for the reader. And finally my wife, daughter and son have endured the process of the book's creation with general good humor and only occasional exasperation, the latter usually serving as a goad to action when I might otherwise have faltered.

For data from which the various sections of the book are

Original interior, Tivoli Brewery, Denver

constructed, I am grateful, first, to the staffs of the Historic American Engineering Record, the Historic American Buildings Survey, and the Prints and Documents Division of the Library of Congress. Many of the pictures and many of the facts compiled for the book have been procured with the help of these organizations. For material on specific sites I am indebted to others, as follows: *Out of the Earth:* T. Alan Comp; Elizabeth Walton, Parks Historian, Oregon State Highway Division; Mrs. Marion B. Atkins, Photographs Librarian, Oklahoma Historical Society; Emory Kemp; Stephen L. Carr, M.D., Utah Historical Society. *From Plants and Animals:* Dianne Newell; Merrill W. Koppe; Jim McGuire, FAR-MAR-Co., Hutchinson, Kansas; James A. Bohart, Chamber of Commerce, Abilene Kansas; William H. Pierson, Jr. *Power and Services:* United States Bureau of Reclamation. *Manufacturing:* Ed Battison and Robert R. Rhodehamel, both of the American Precision Museum, Windsor, Vermont; Connecticut Historical Society; Colt Industries, Firearms Division, Hartford, Connecticut; Mrs. Helen Deason, Public Relations Manager, Albert Kahn Associates, Detroit, Michigan; The Museum of Modern Art, New York. *Transportation and Communication:* Chester H. Liebs; United States Coast Guard; F. R. Holland, Jr.; Ed Michael, Department of City Planning, San Francisco, California; Manville B. Wakefield; Grant Heilman; Hugh A. Dunne, Electric Railroaders Association.

Information on specific industrial sites listed in Appendix IV, was provided by the Historic American Engineering Record; David Chase, Rhode Island Historical Preservation Commission; Chester H. Liebs; Gary B. Kulik, Slater Mill Historic Site, Pawtucket, Rhode Island.

# Index

Kinzua viaduct (Erie Railroad), Kinzua, Pennsylvania

152